I0482346

The Adult Coloring Book: Mindful Mandalas

By: Adult Coloring Books

ISBN-10: 1534898557
ISBN-13: 978-1534898554

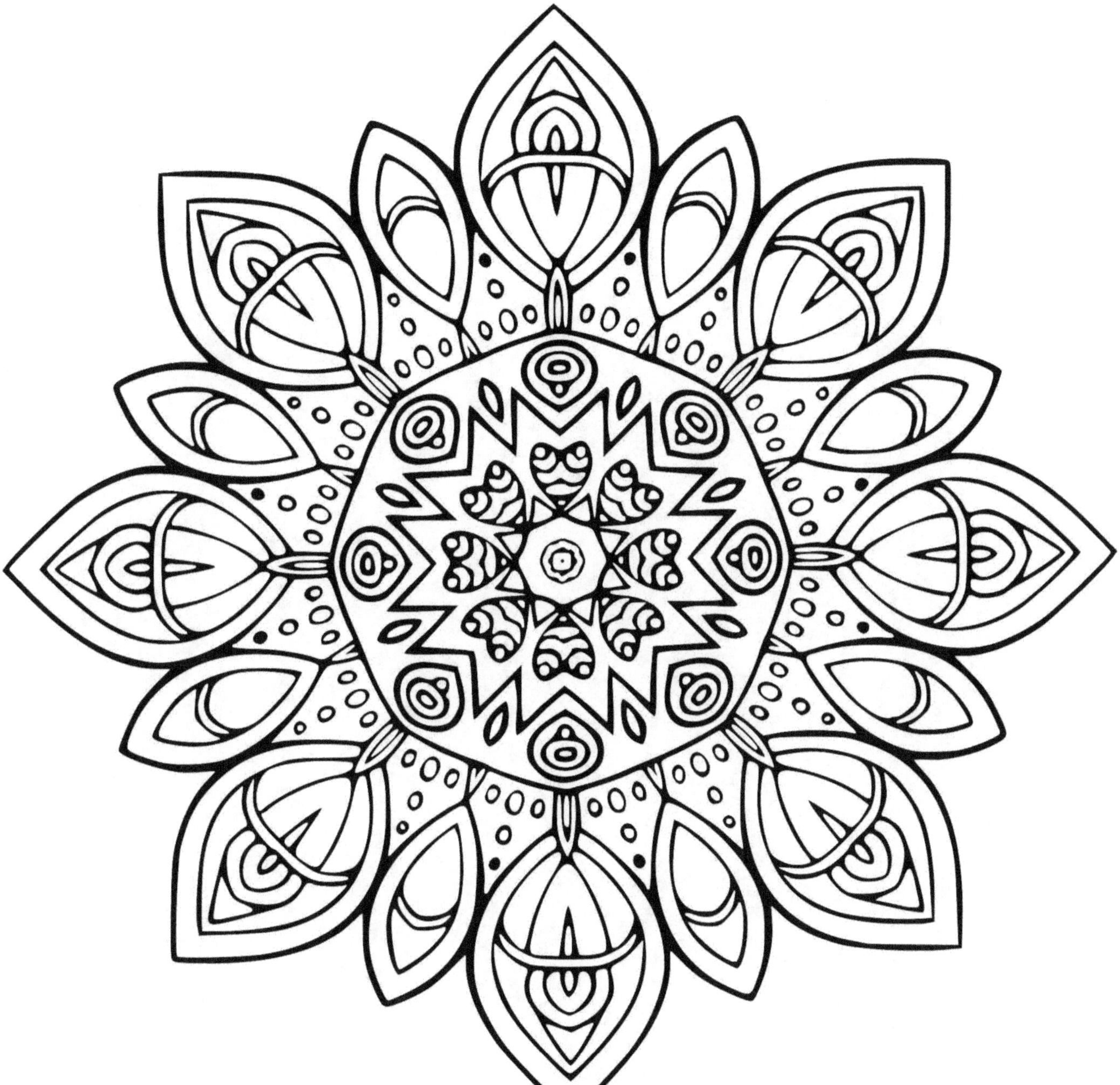

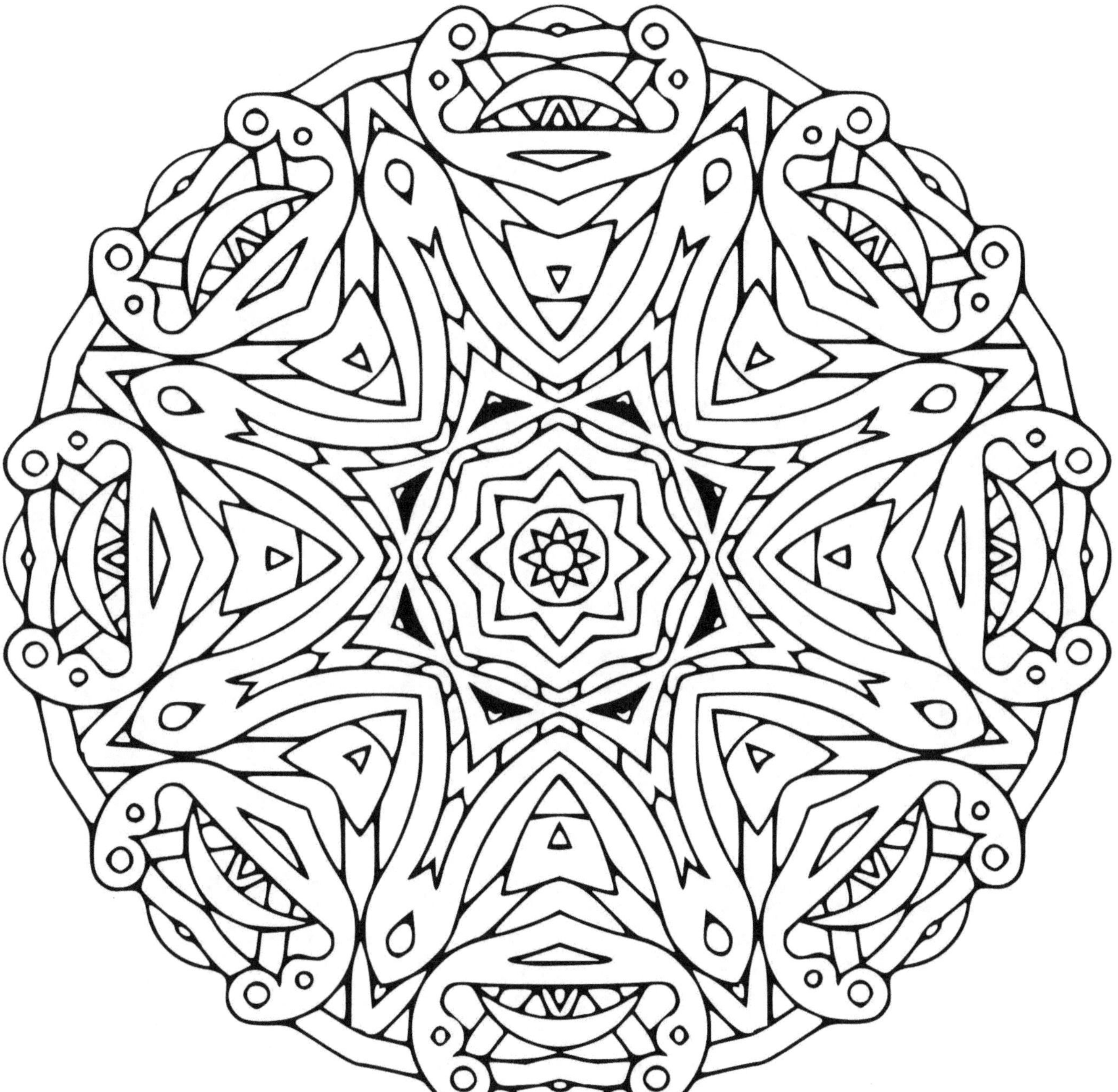

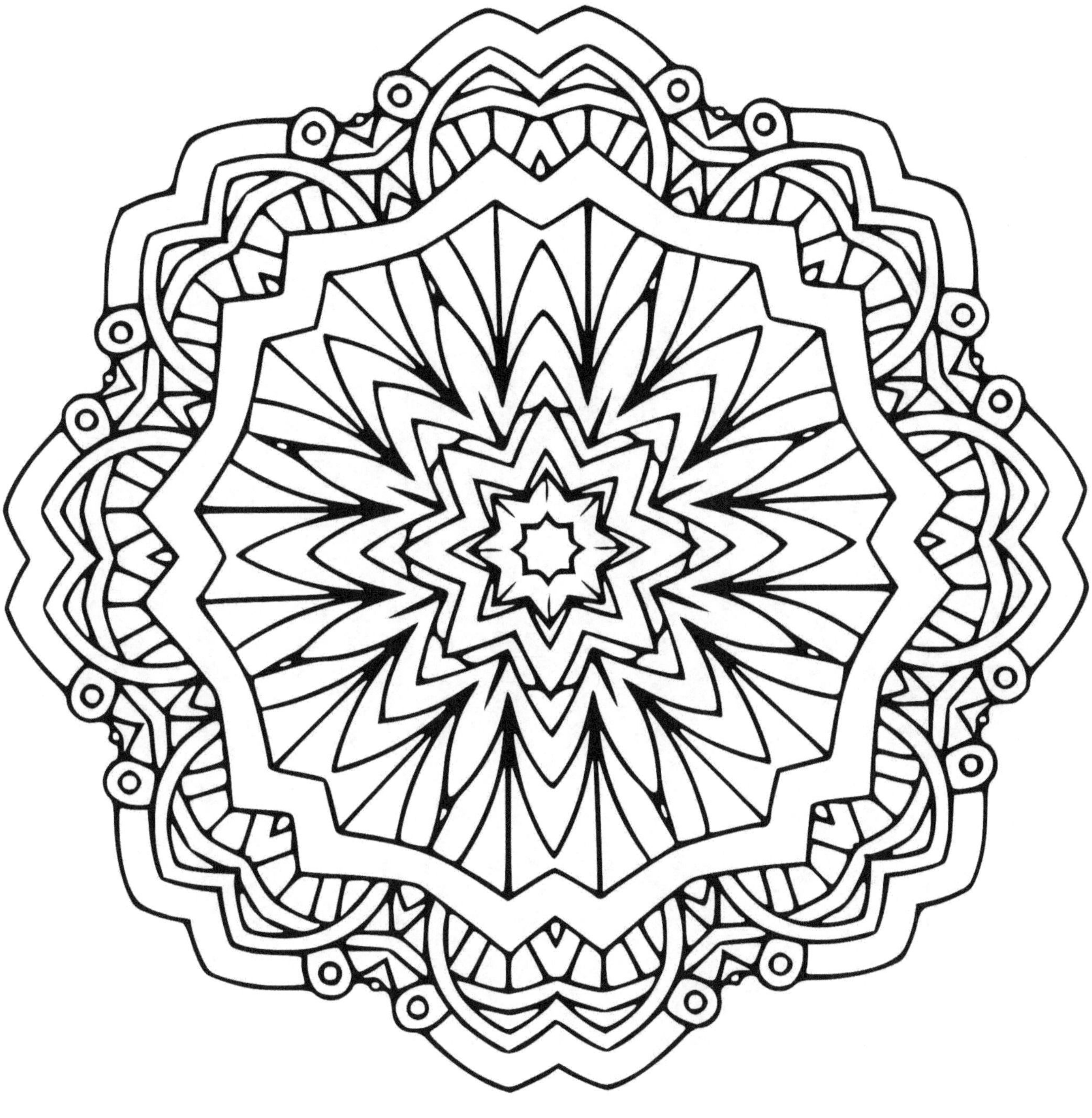

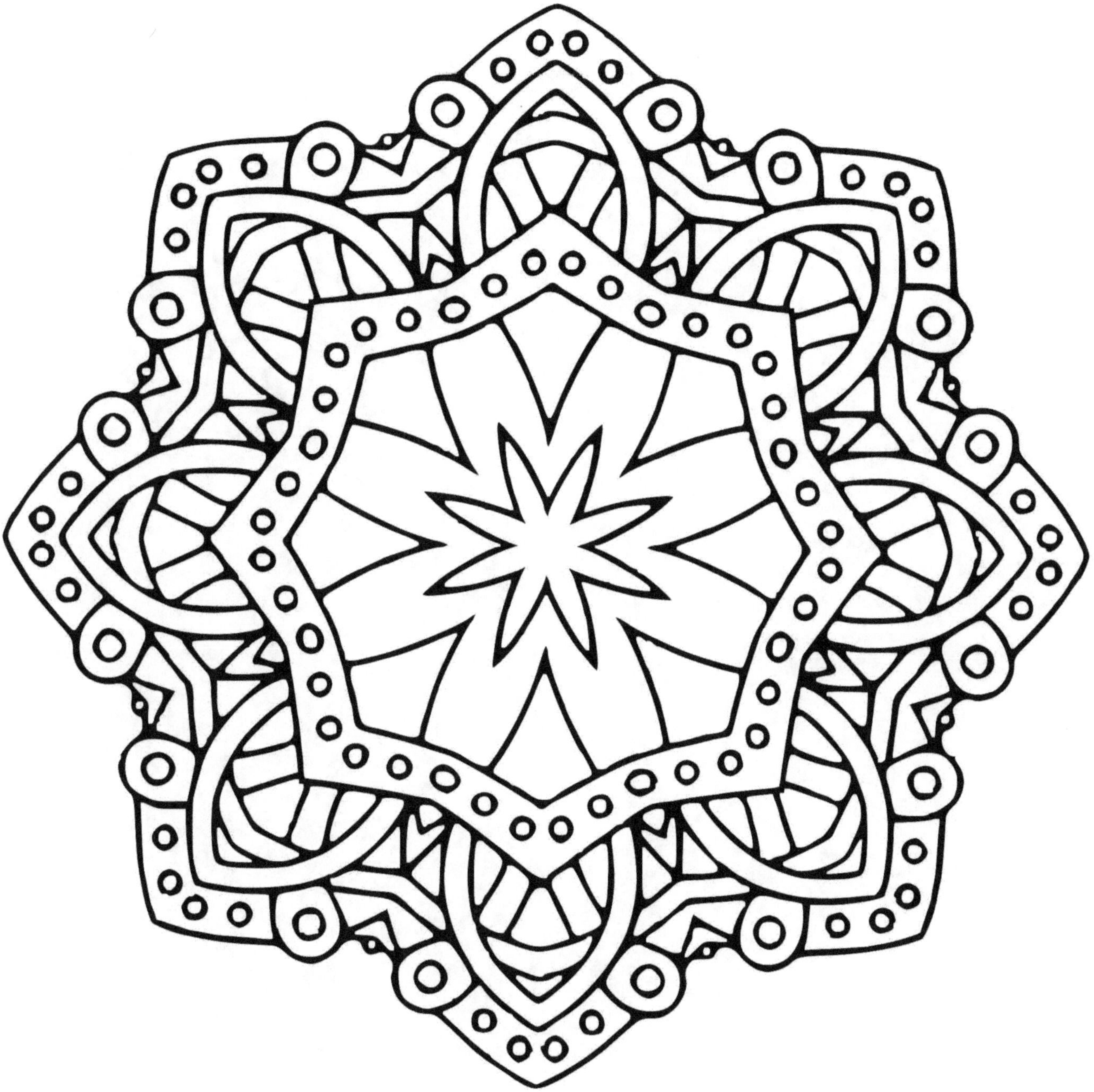

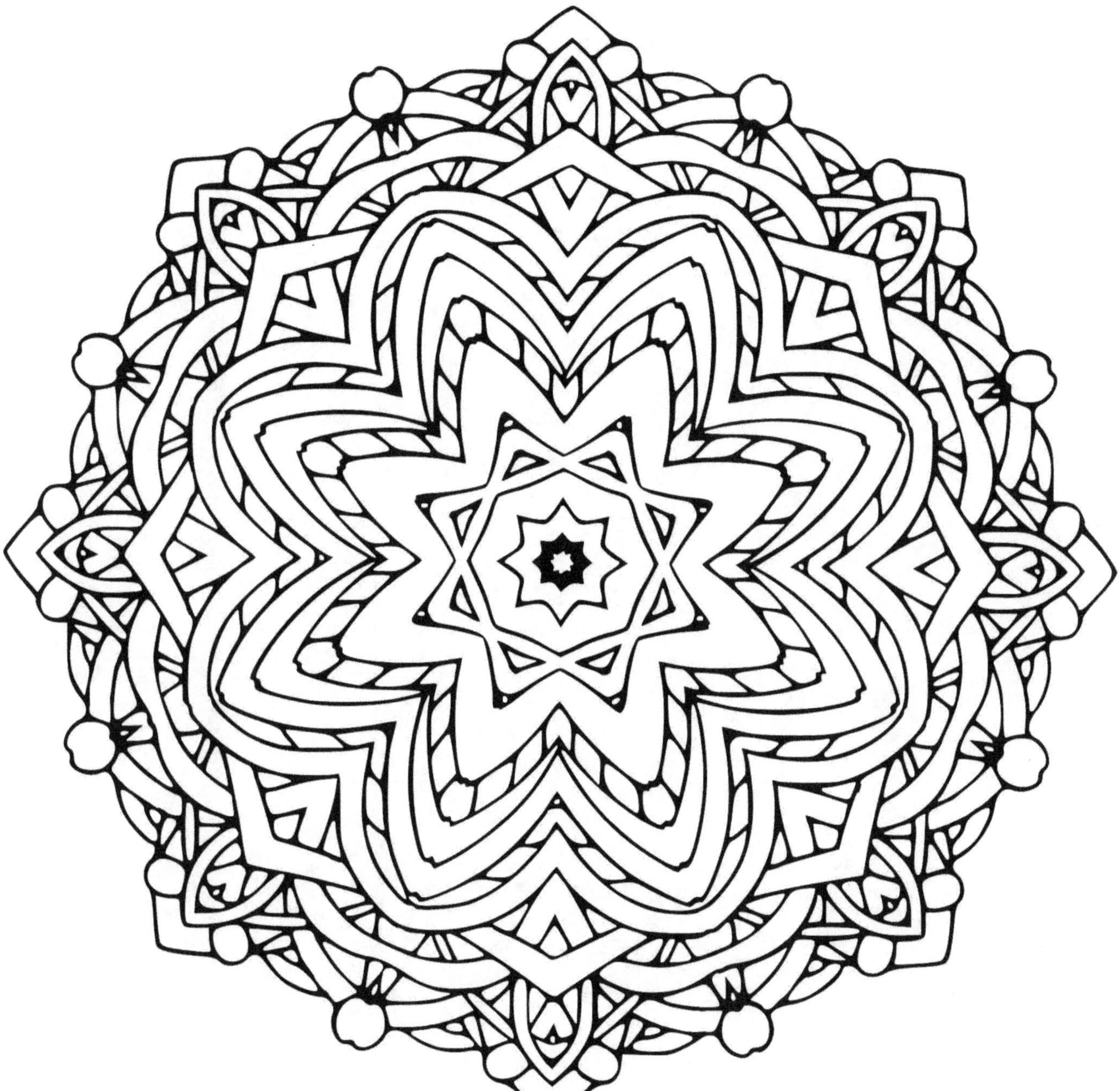

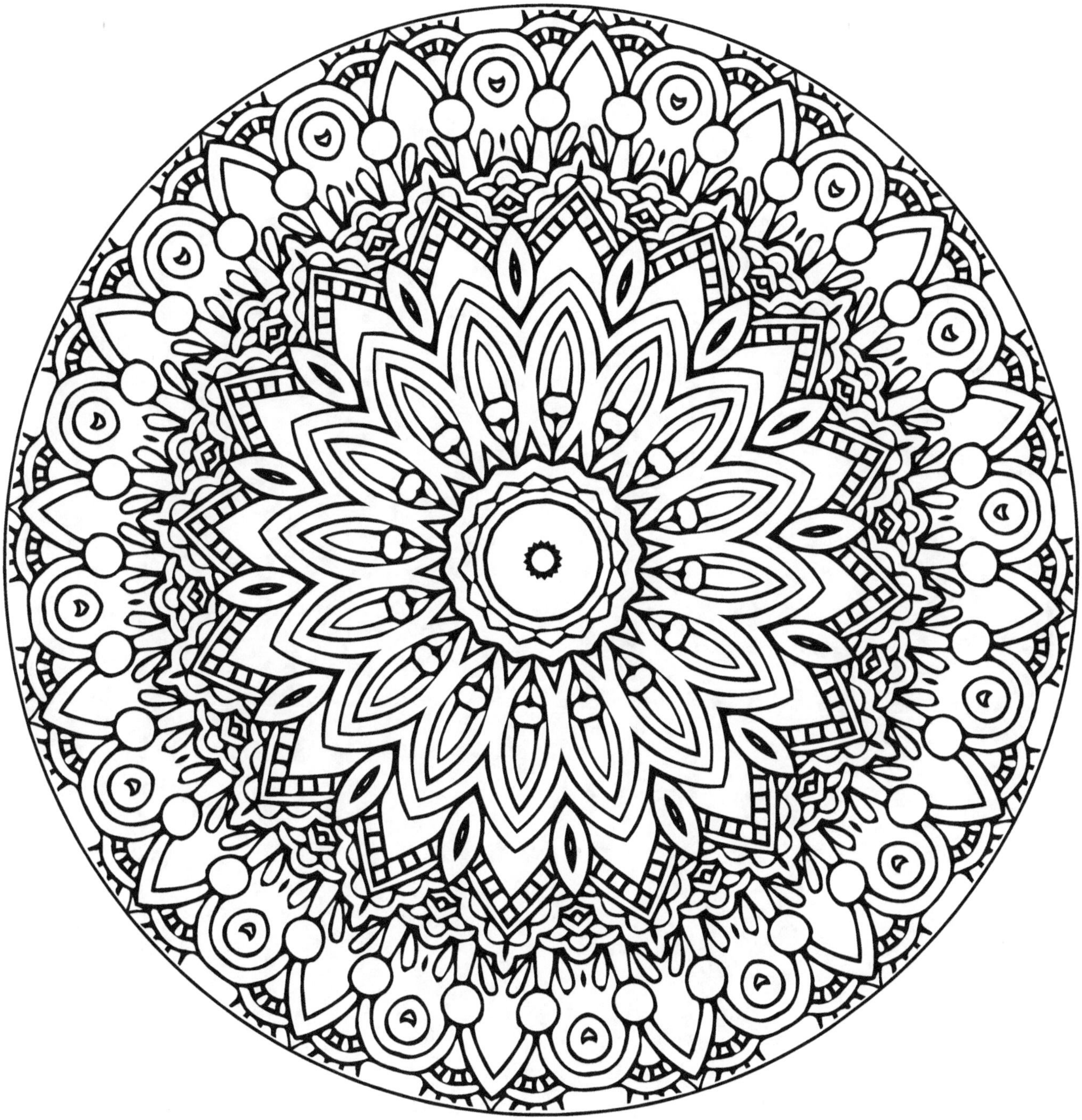

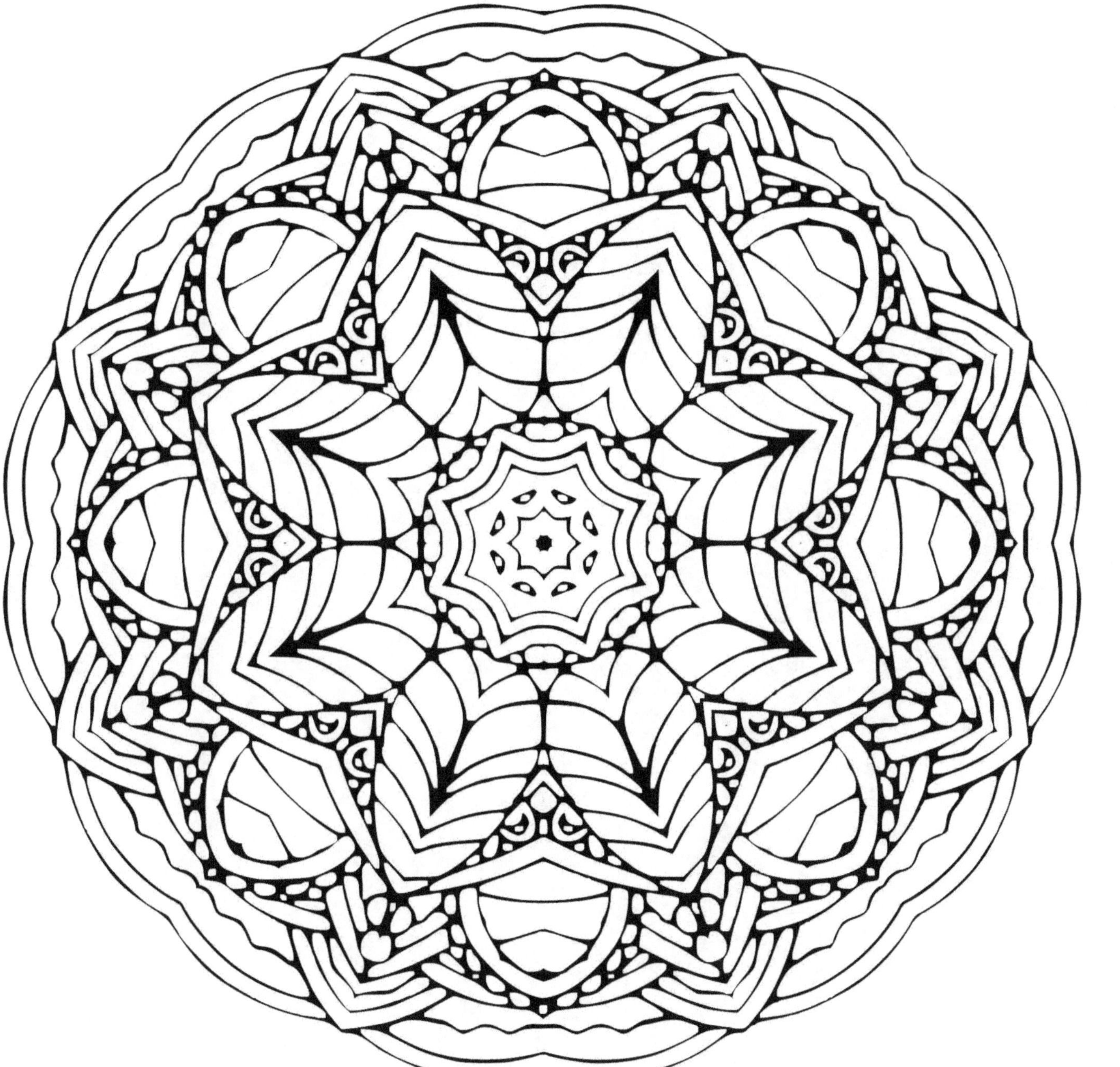

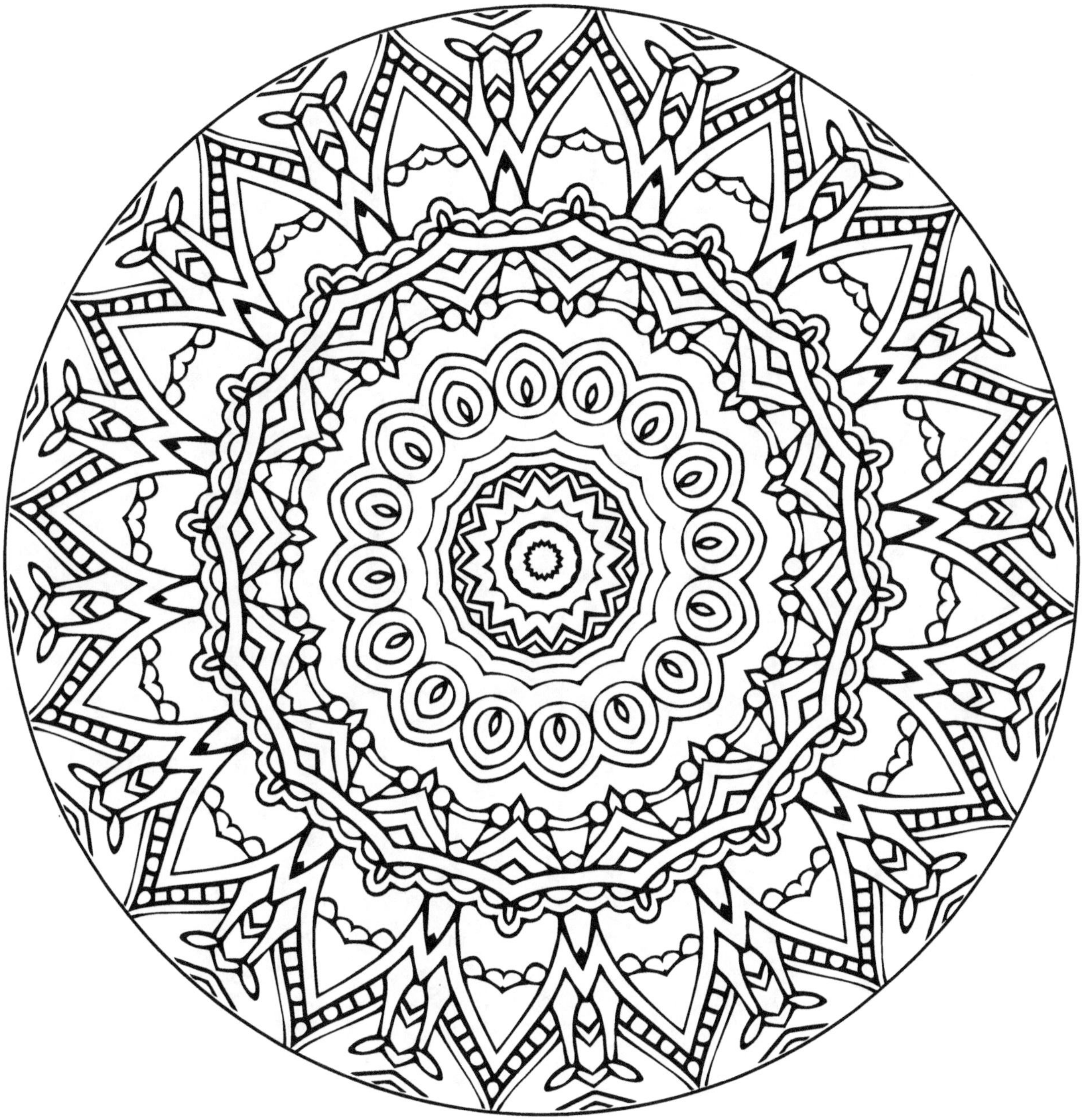

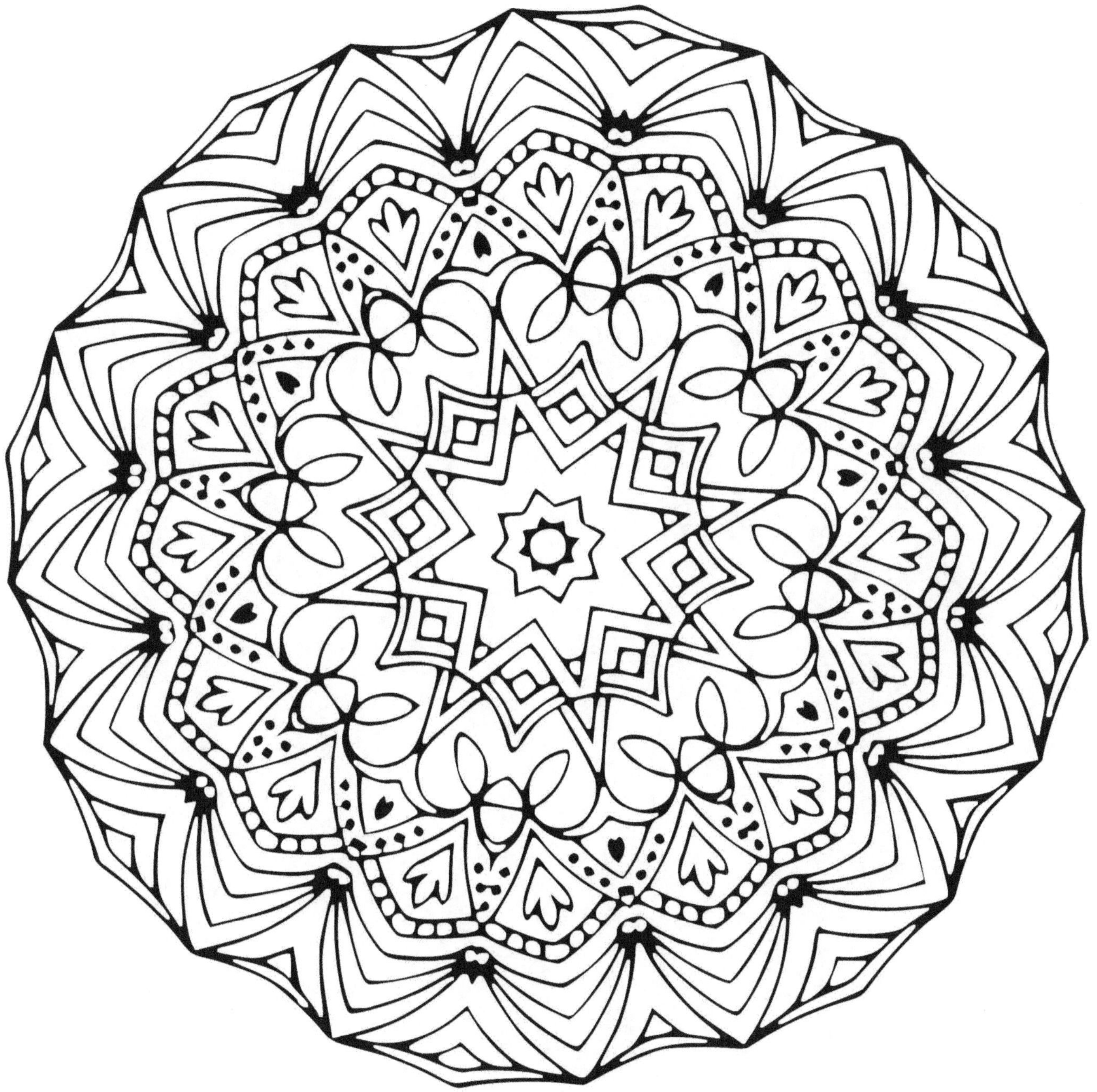

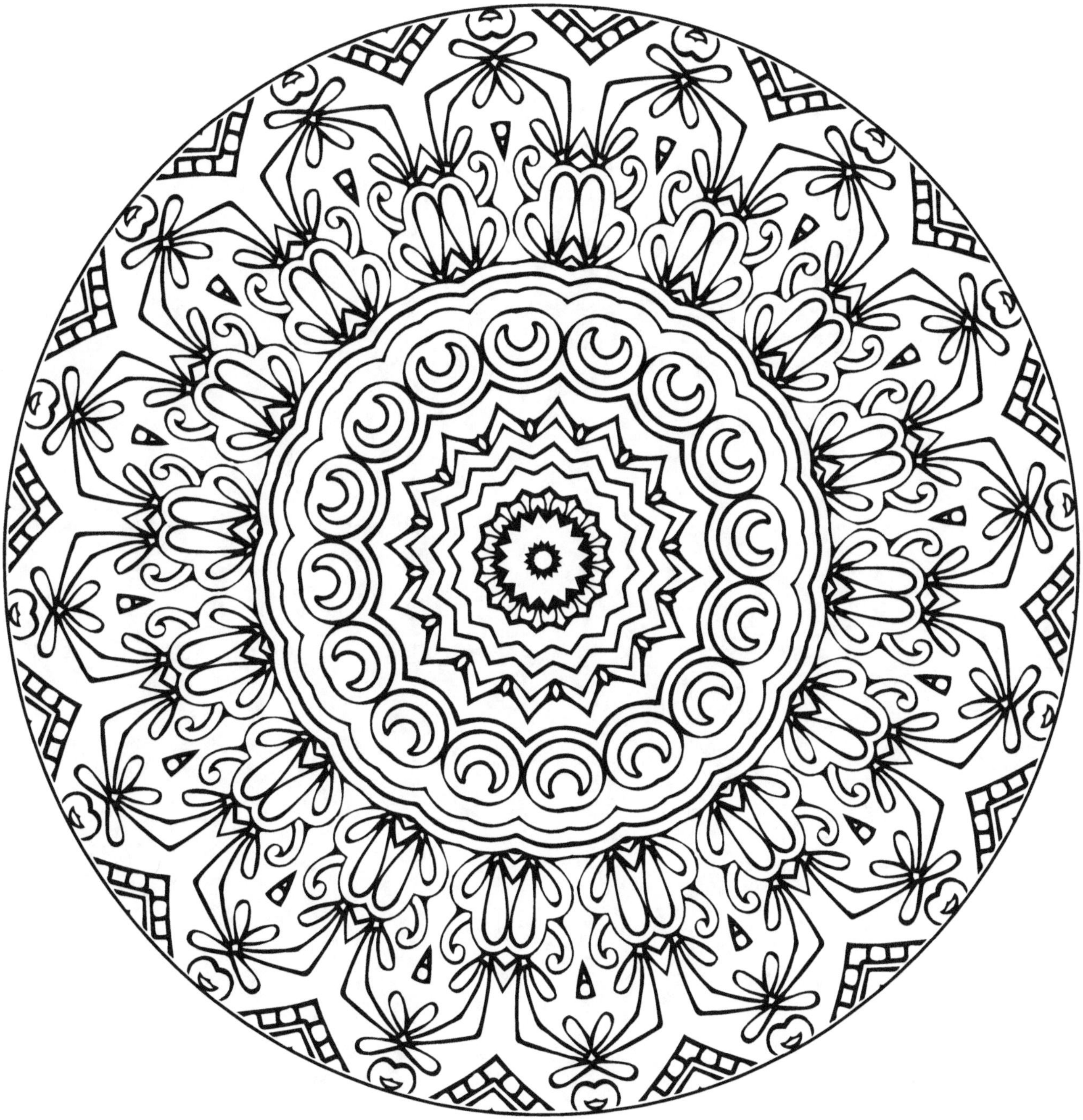

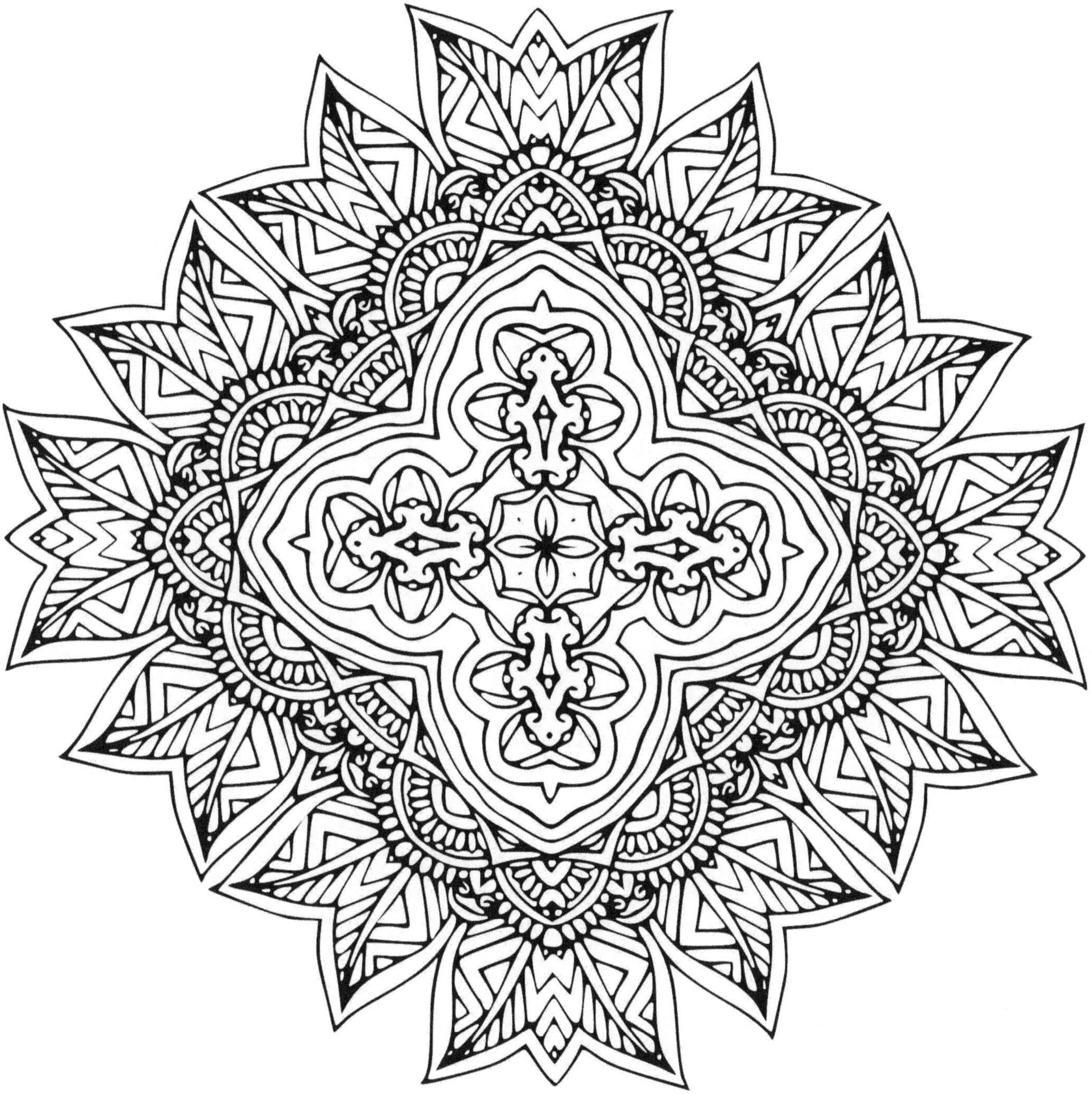

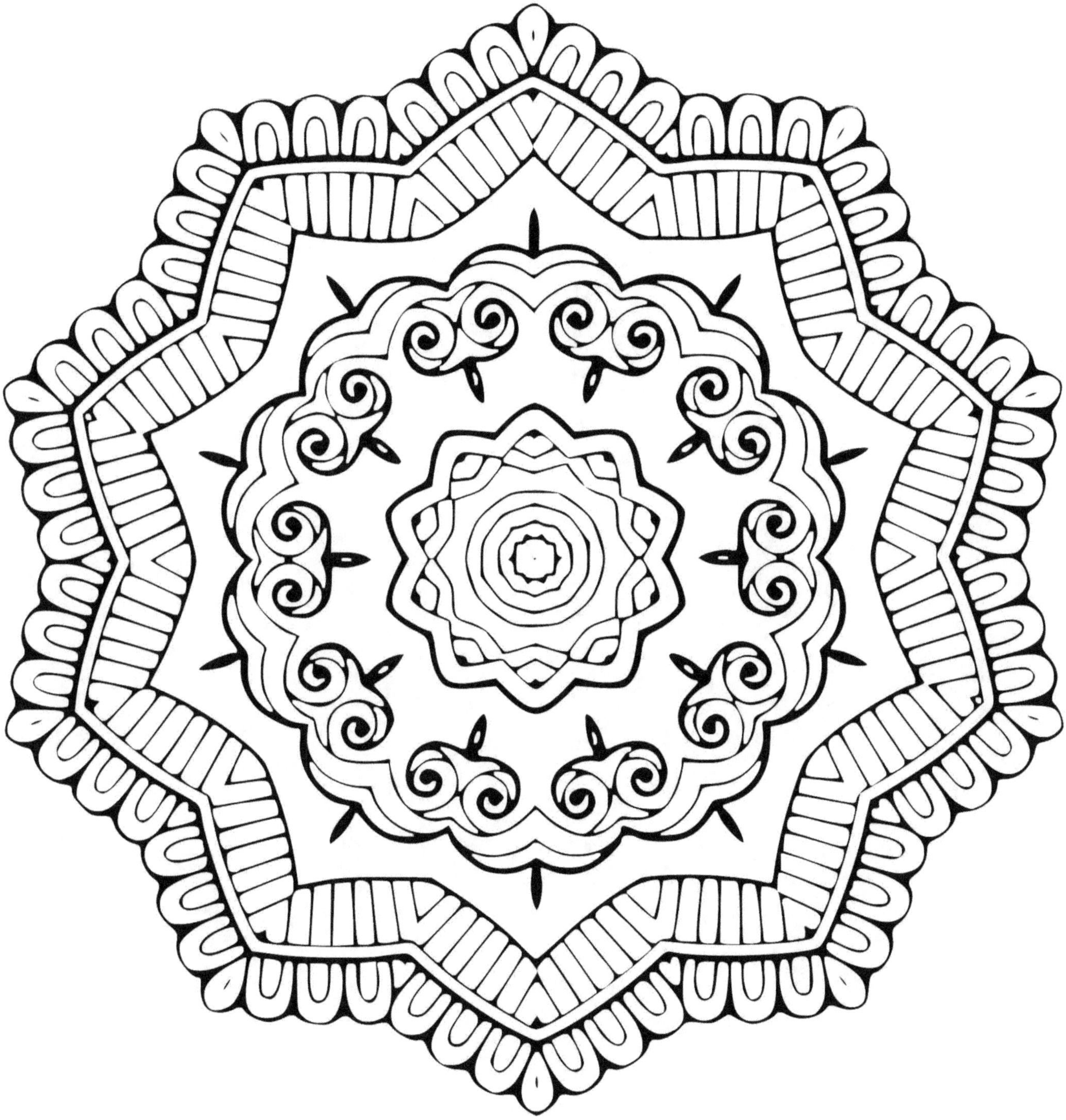

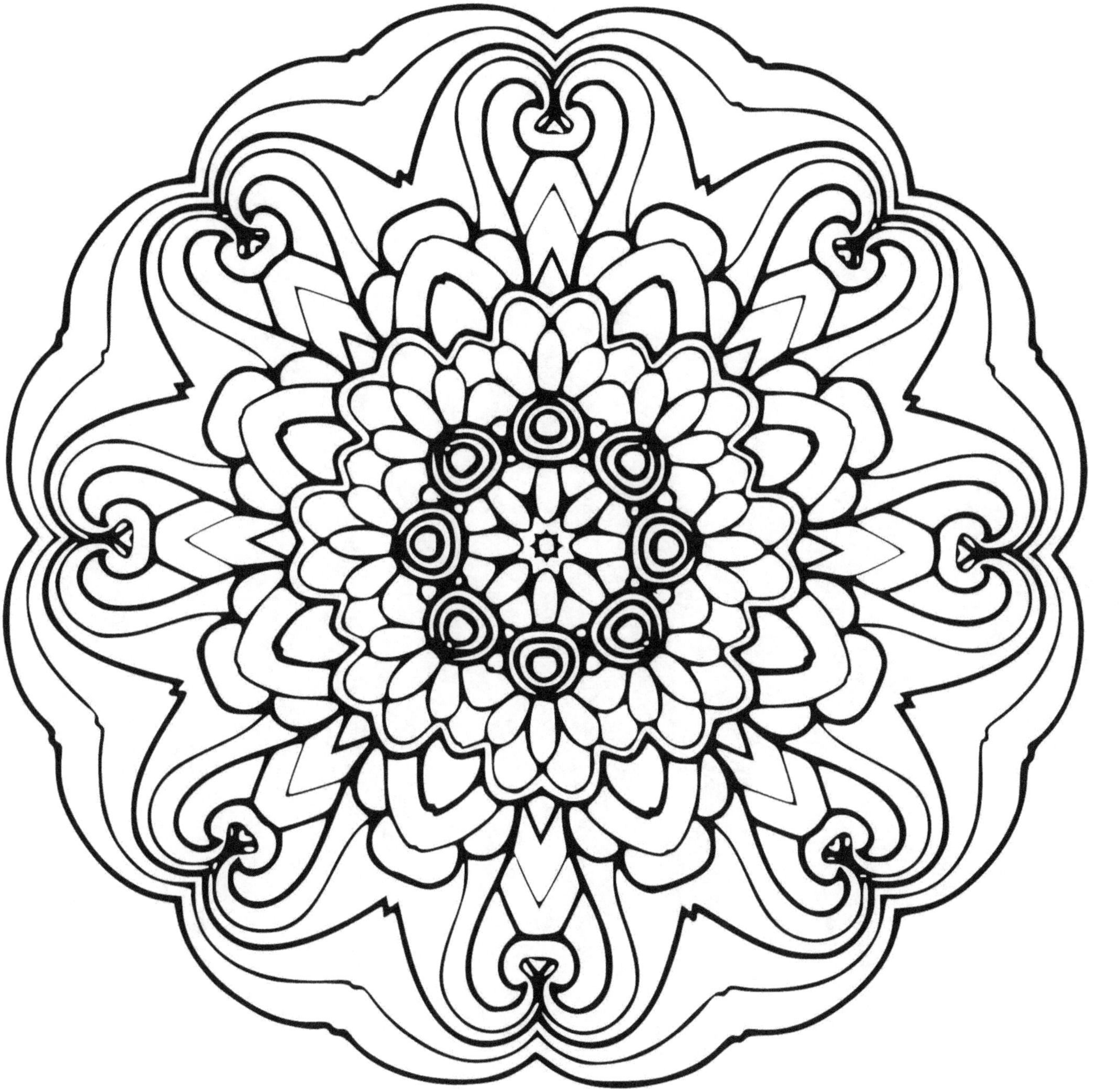

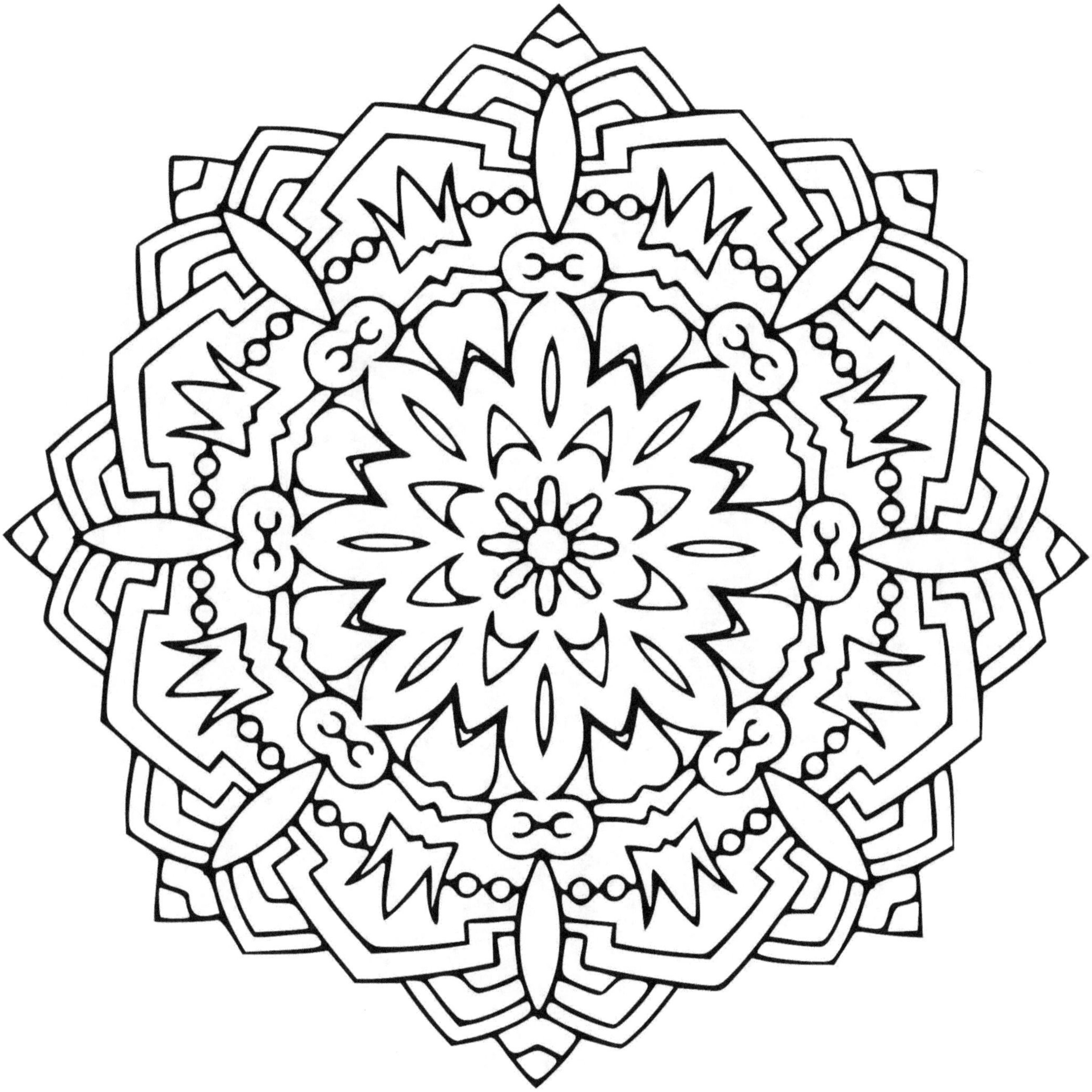

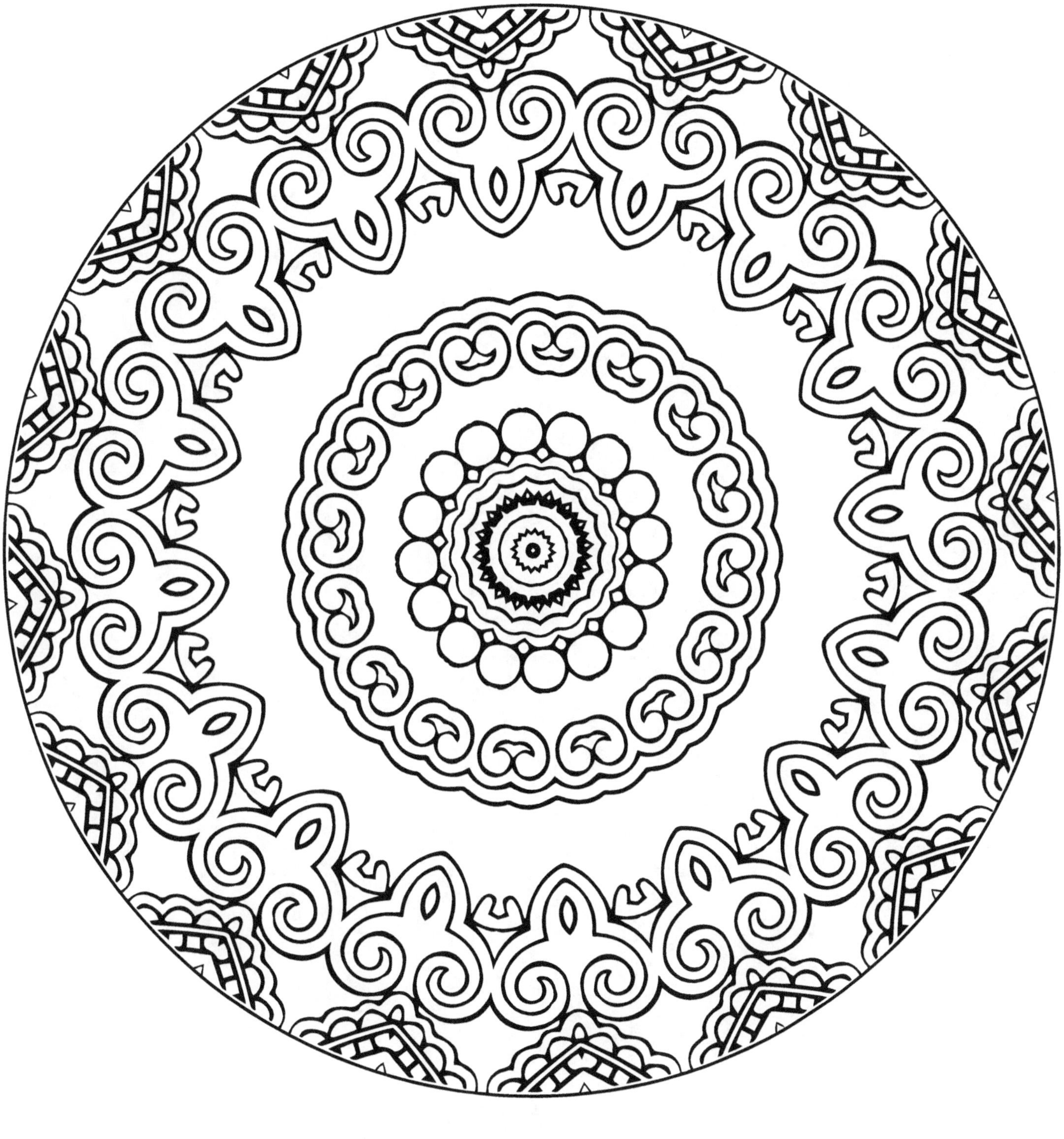

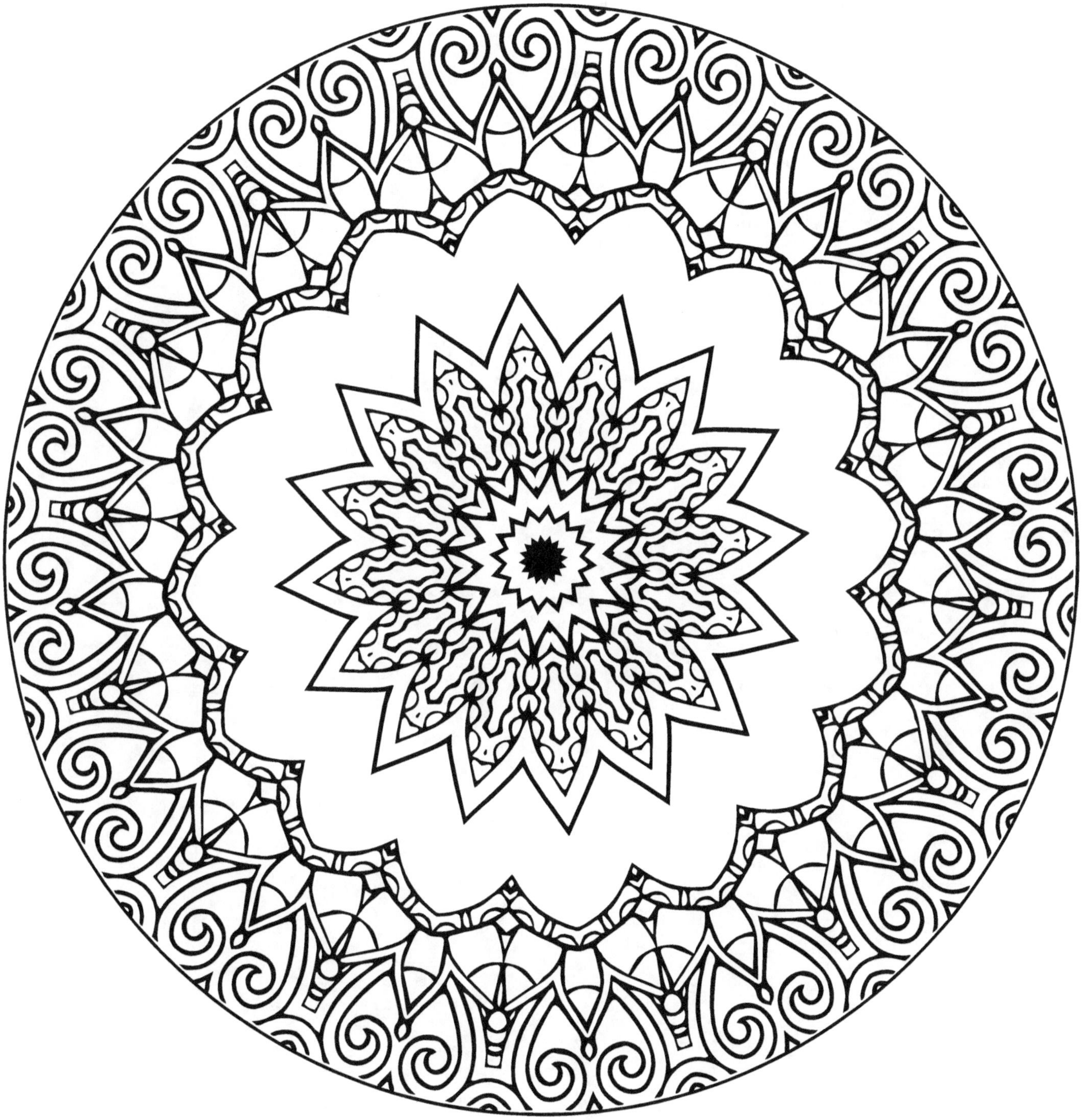

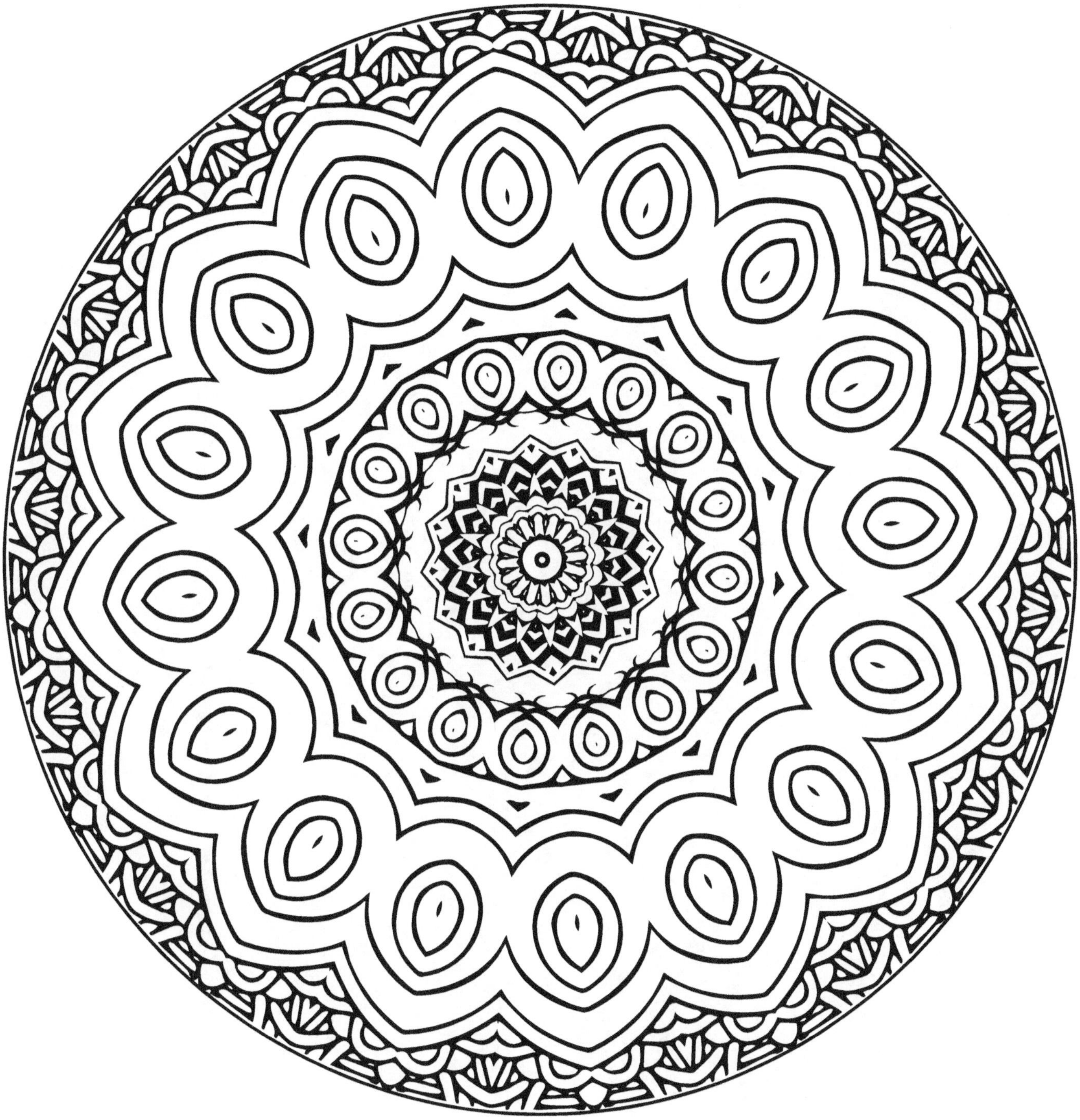

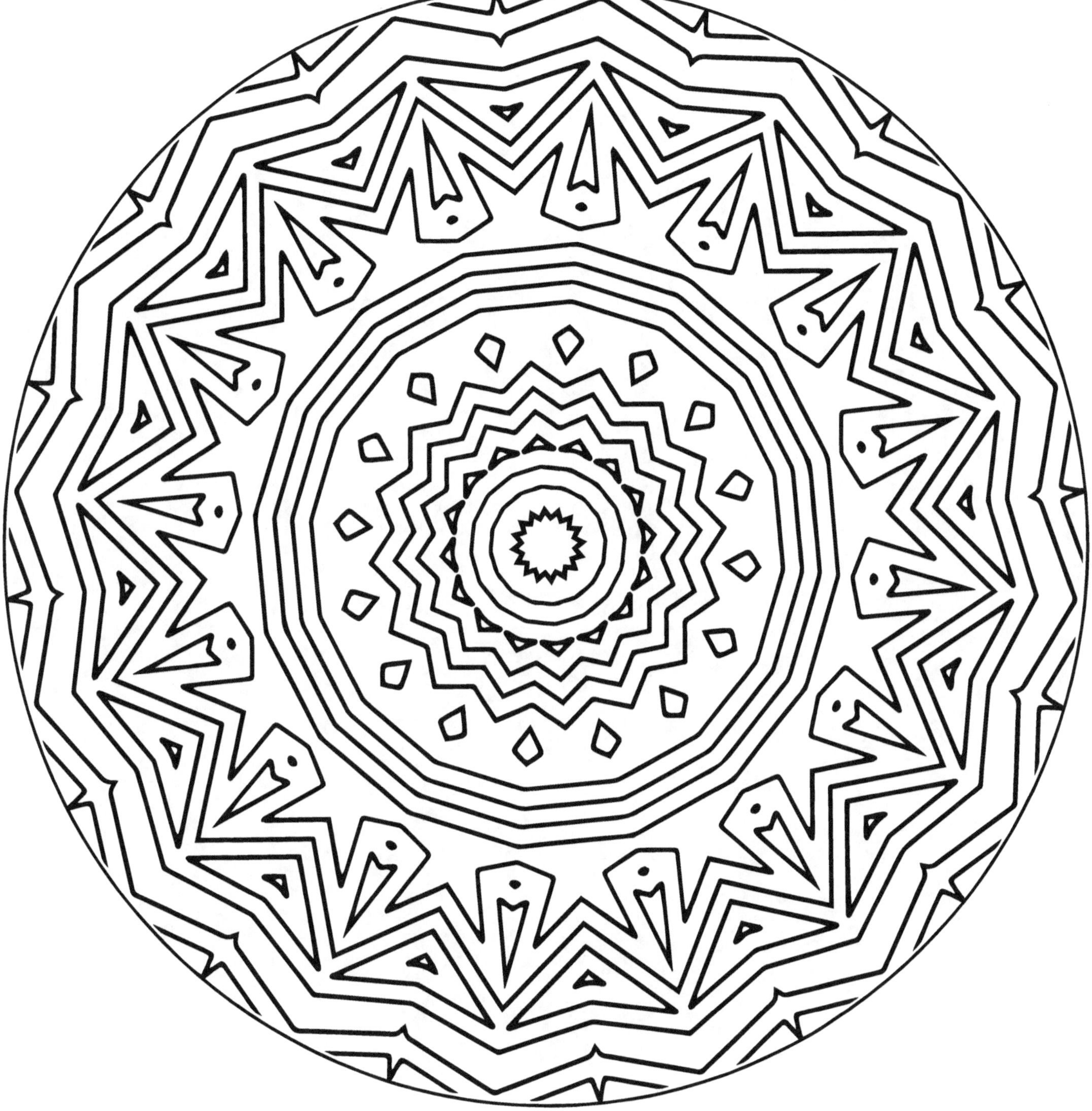

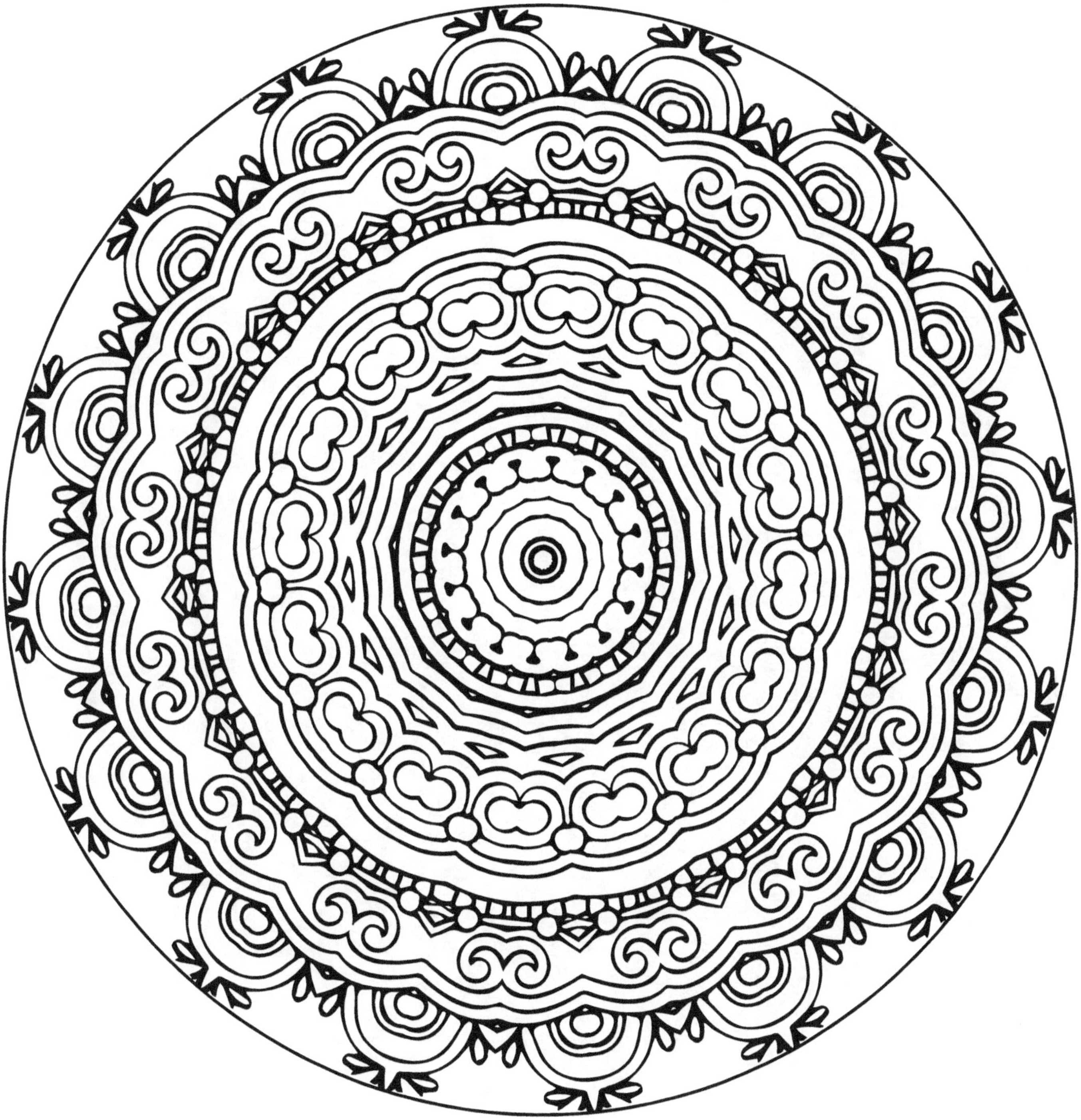

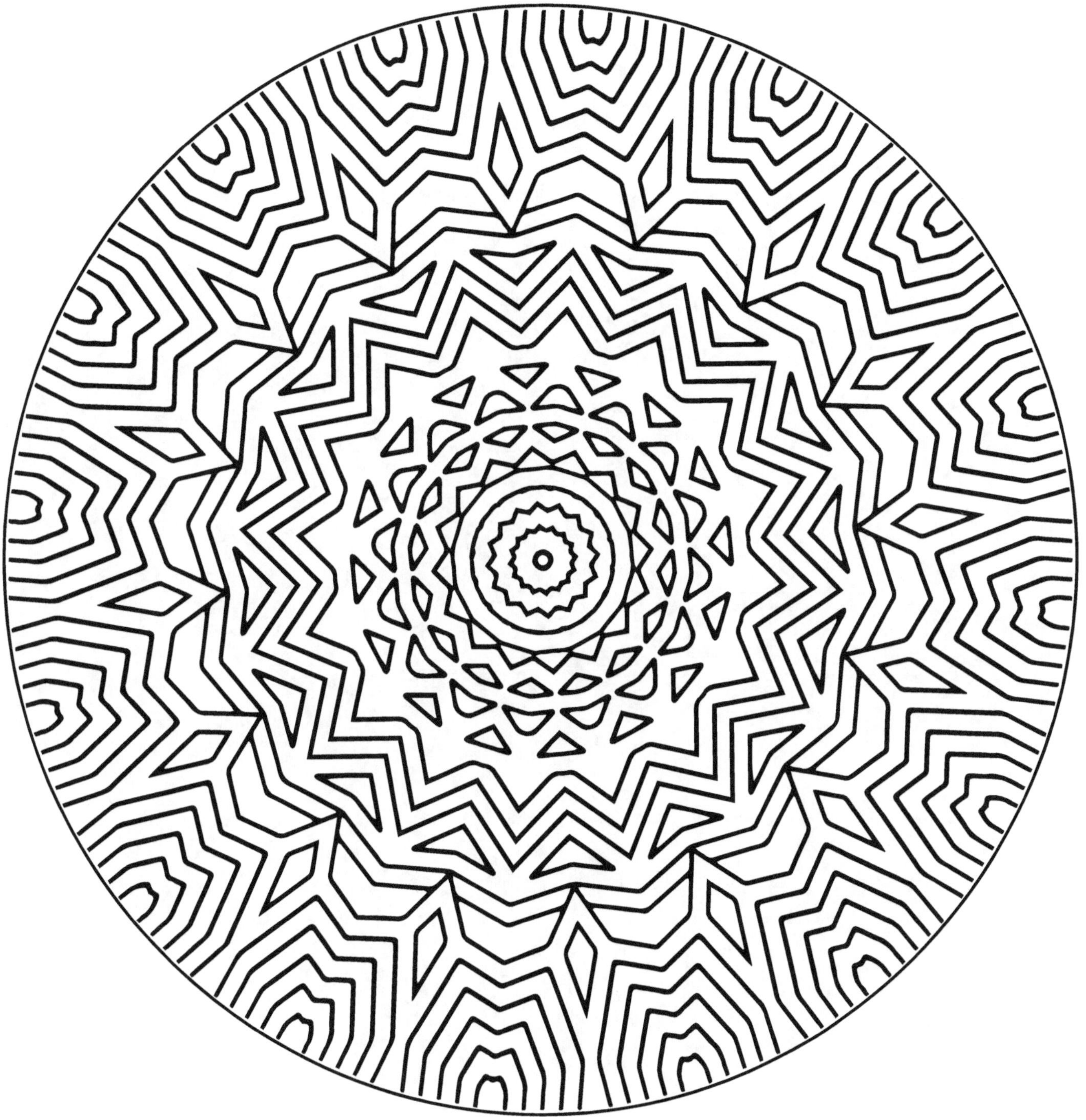

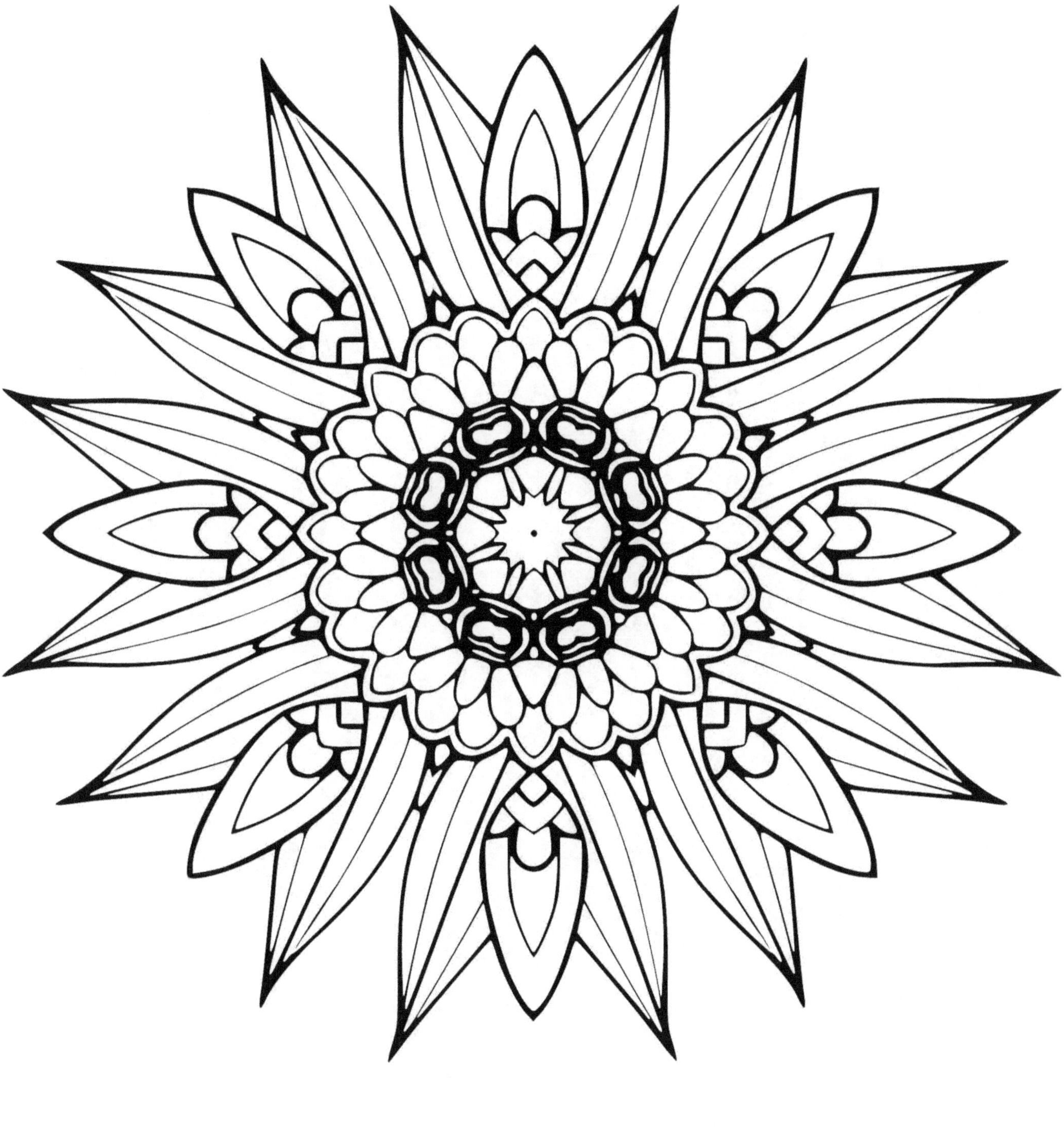

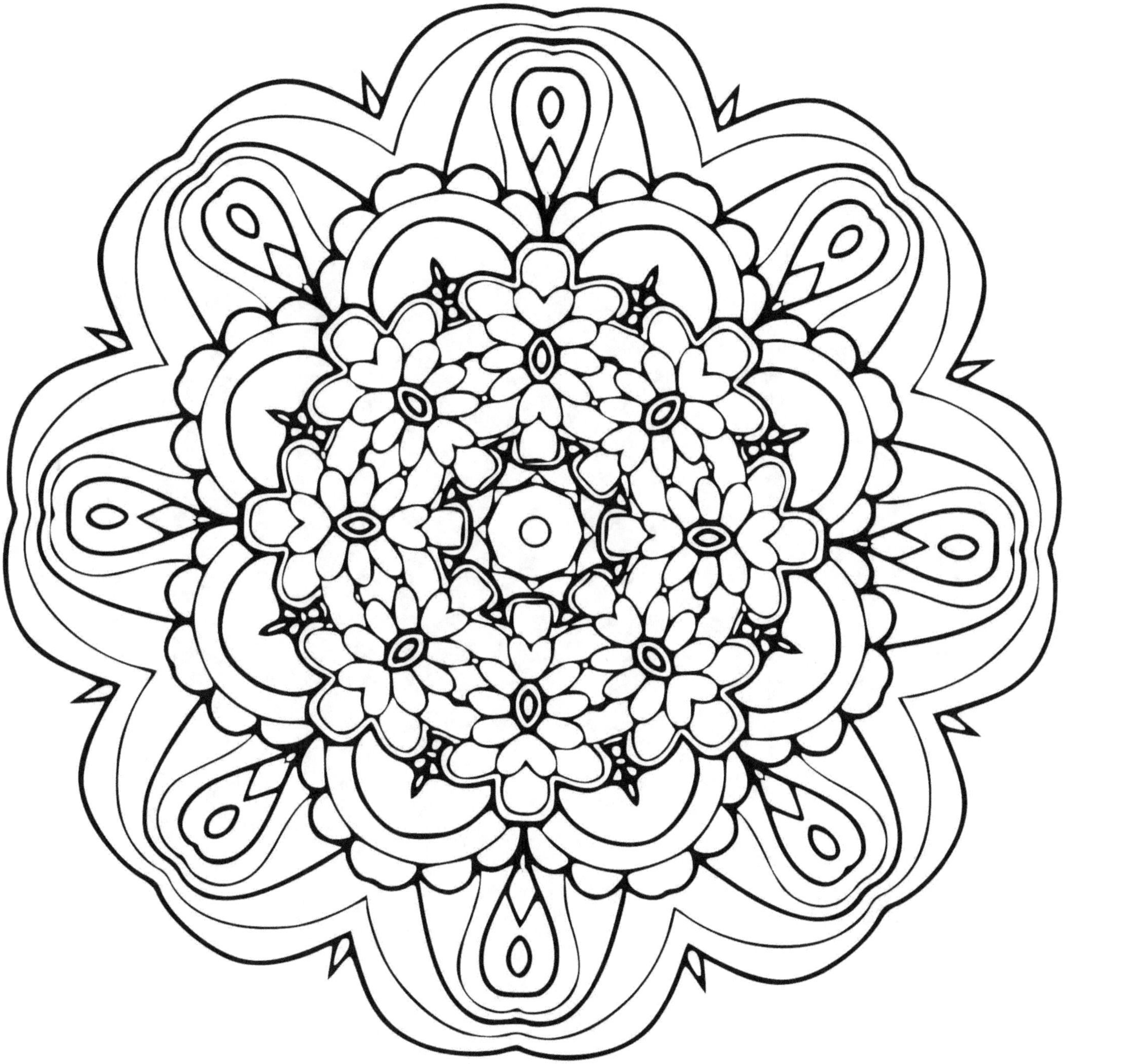

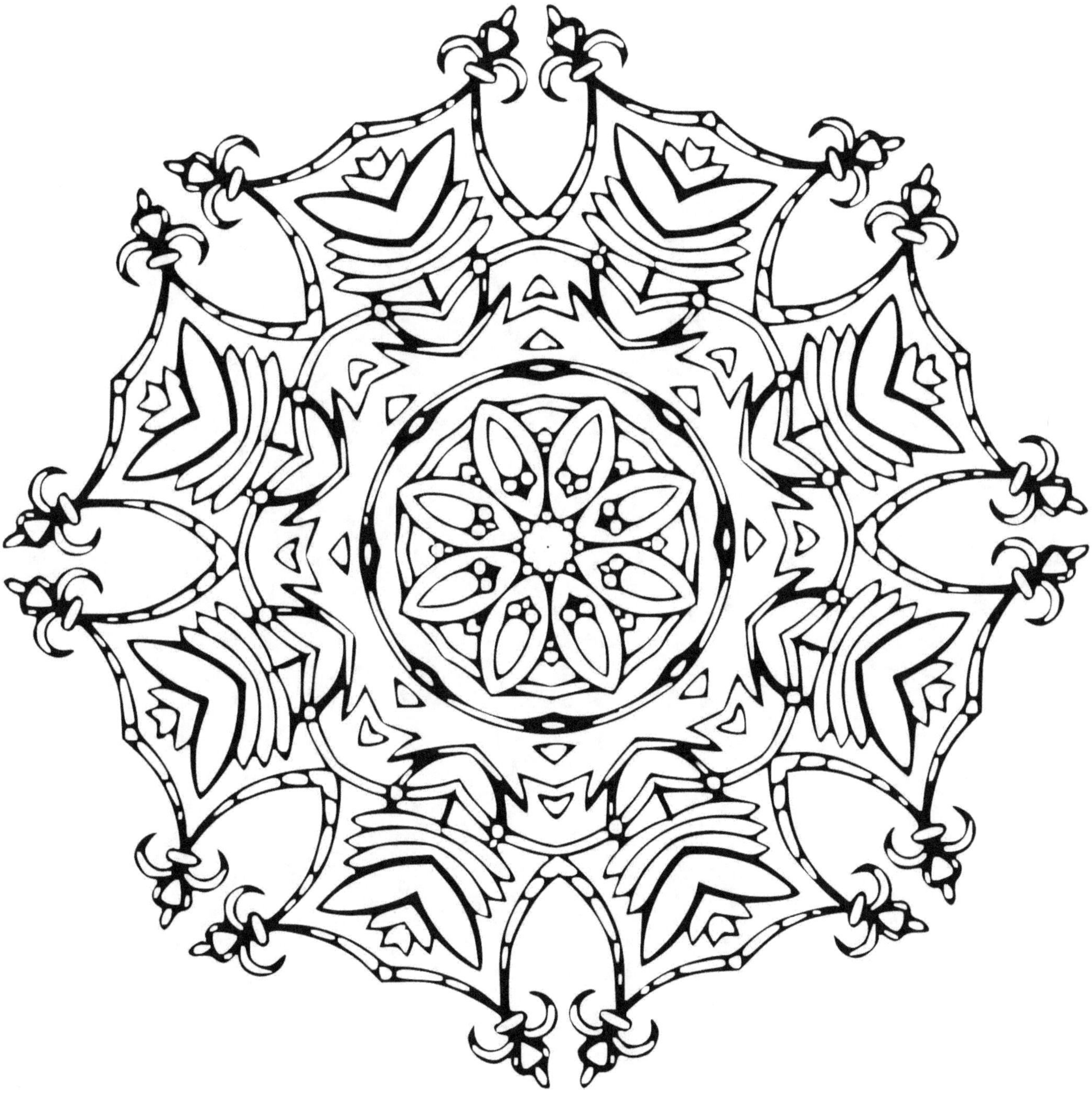

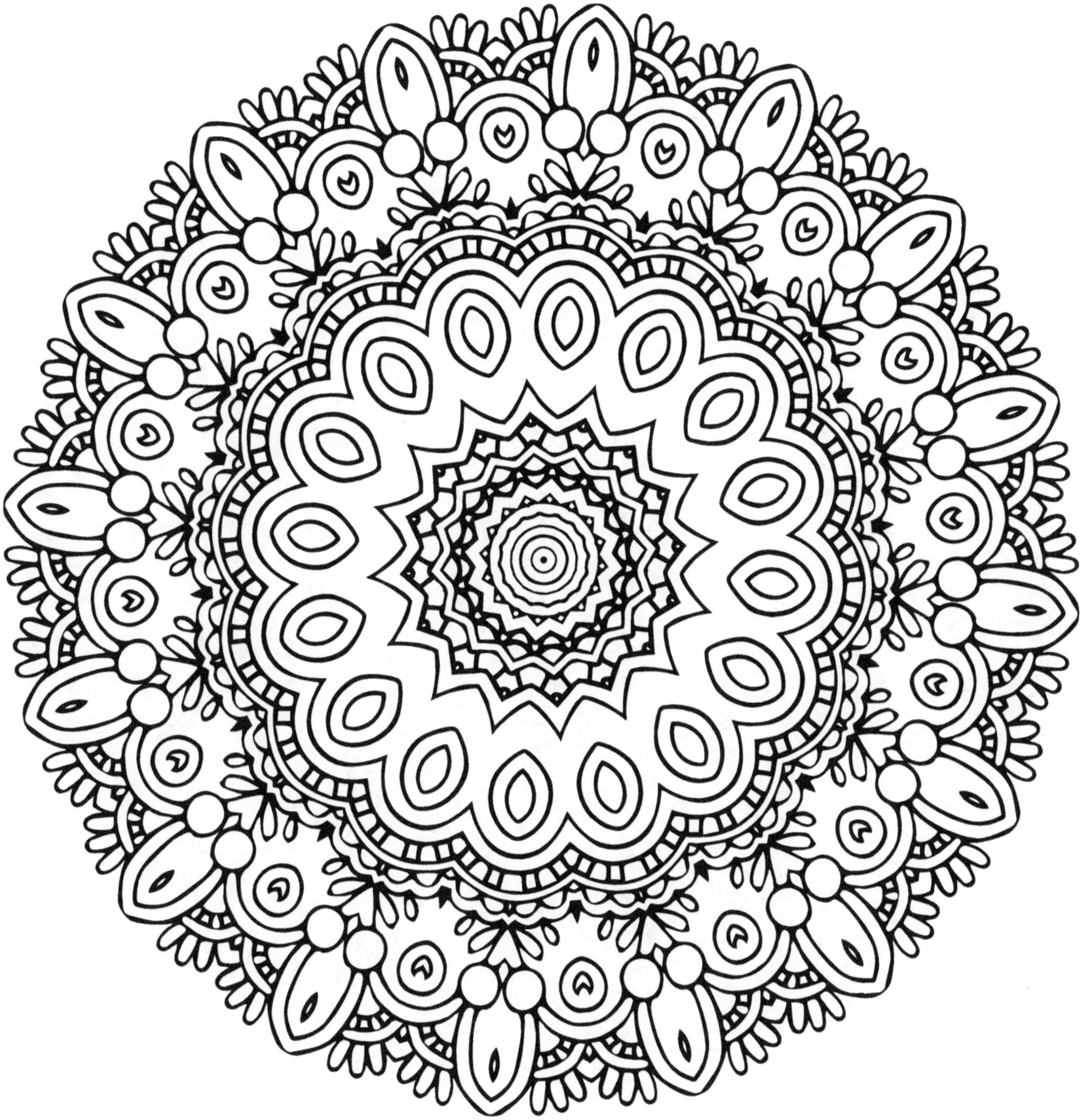

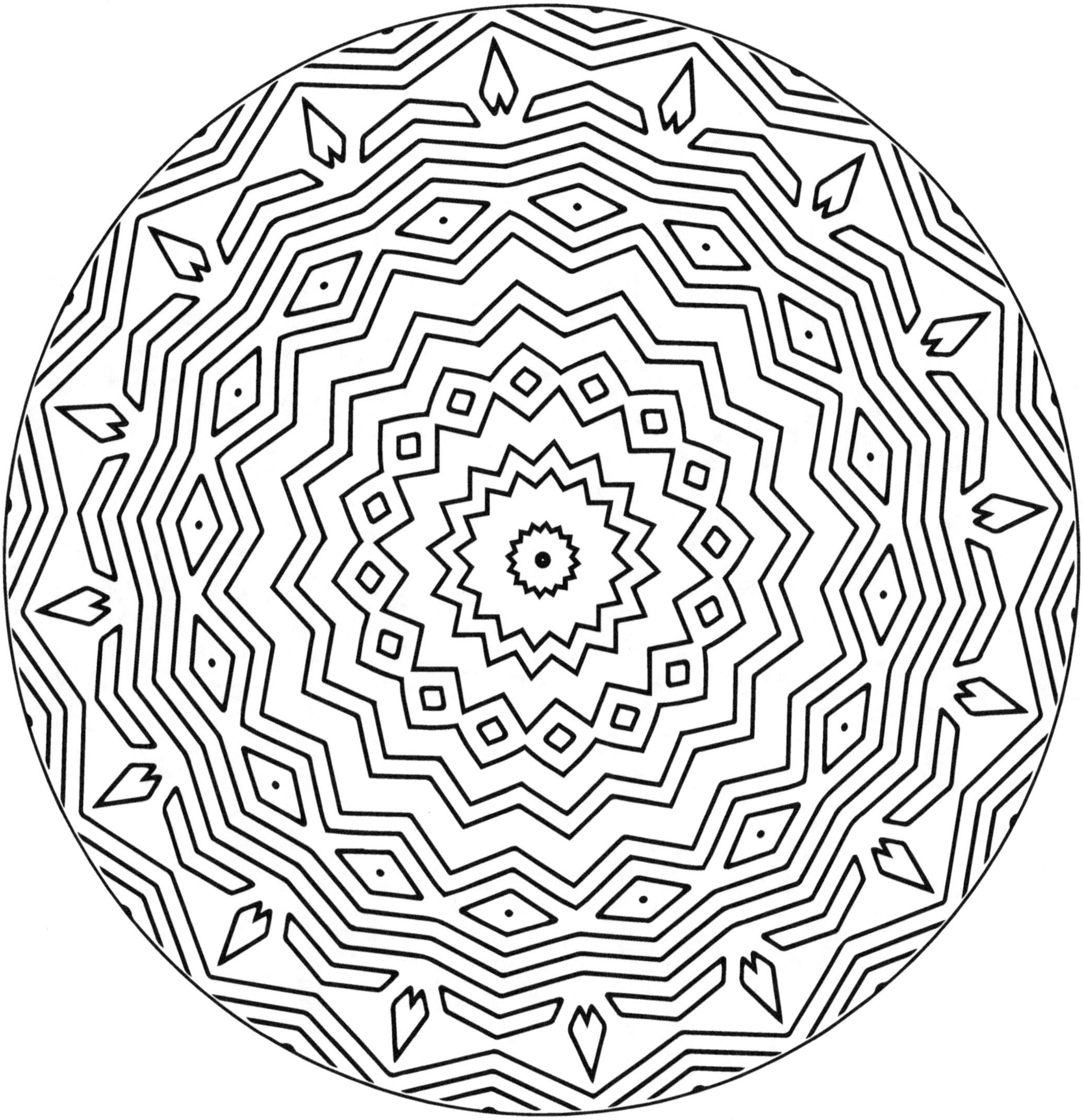

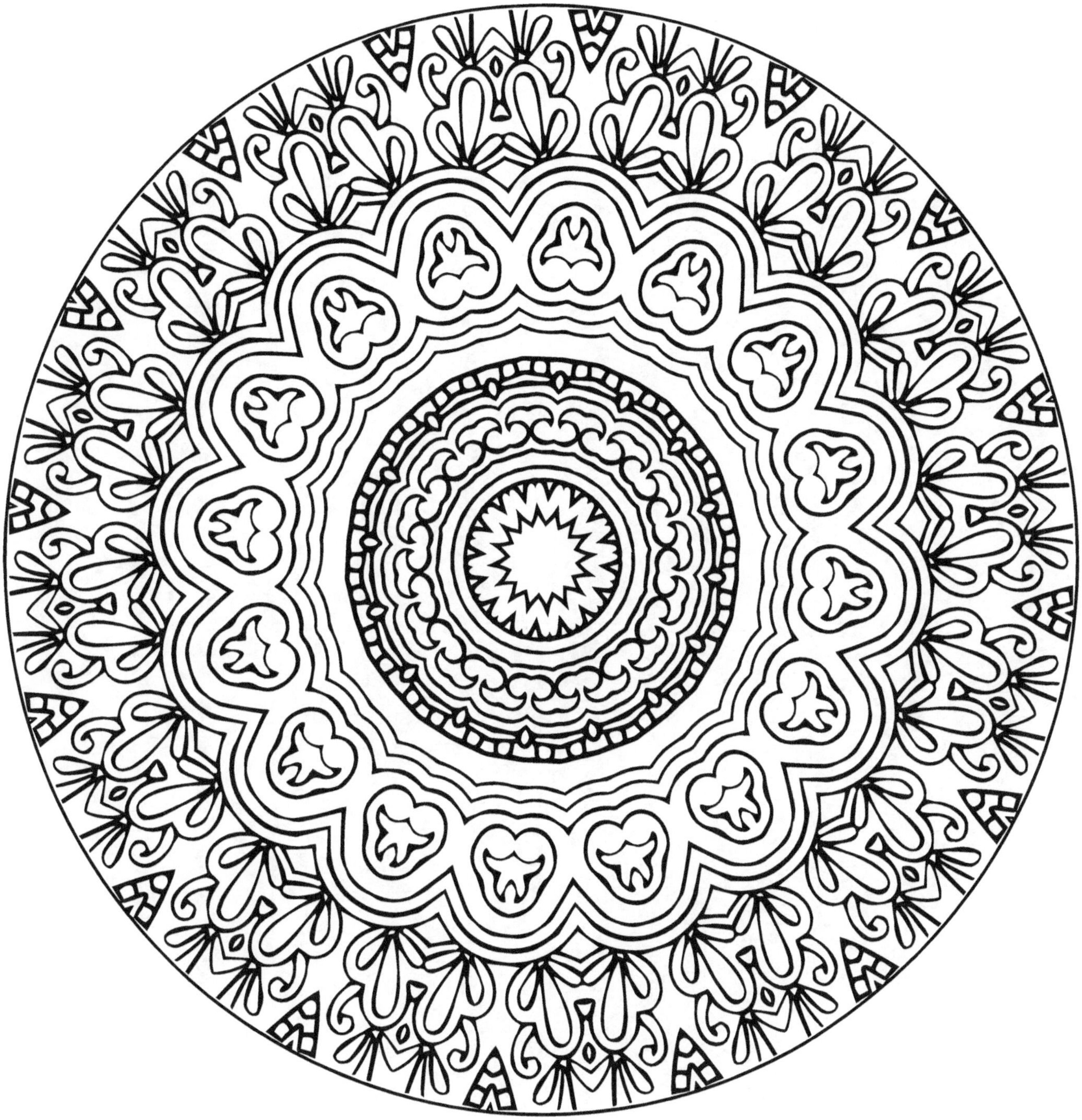

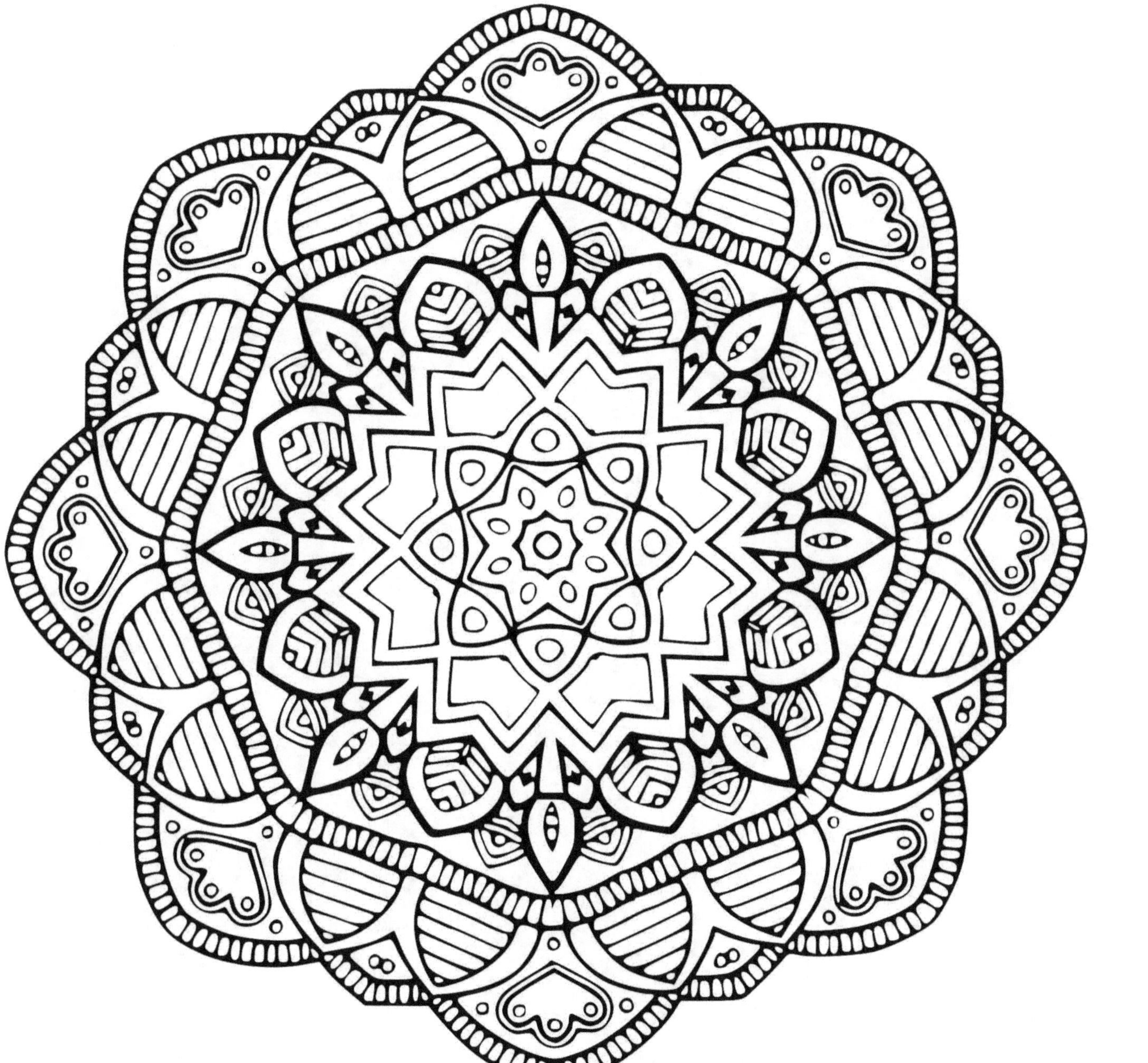

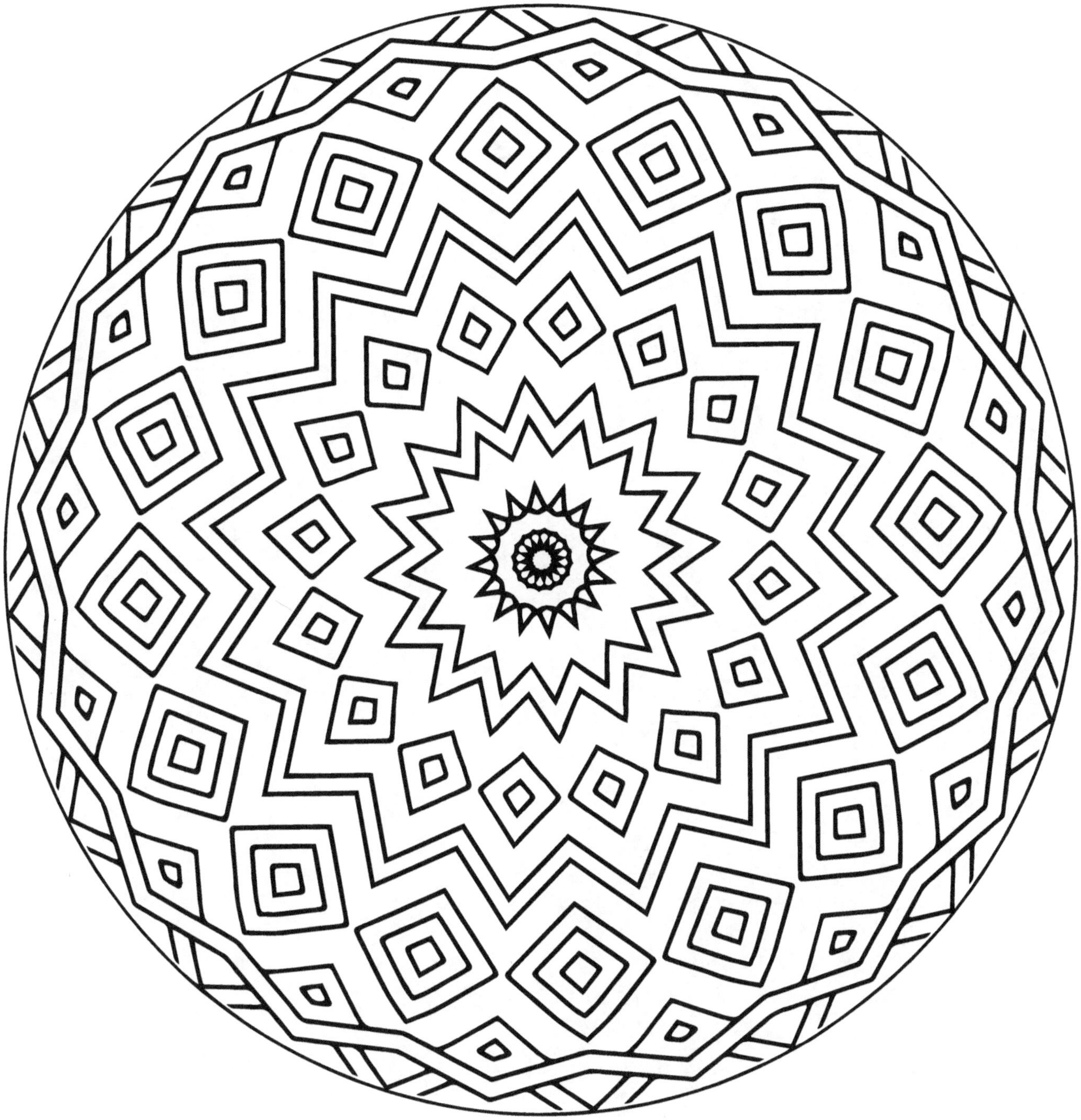

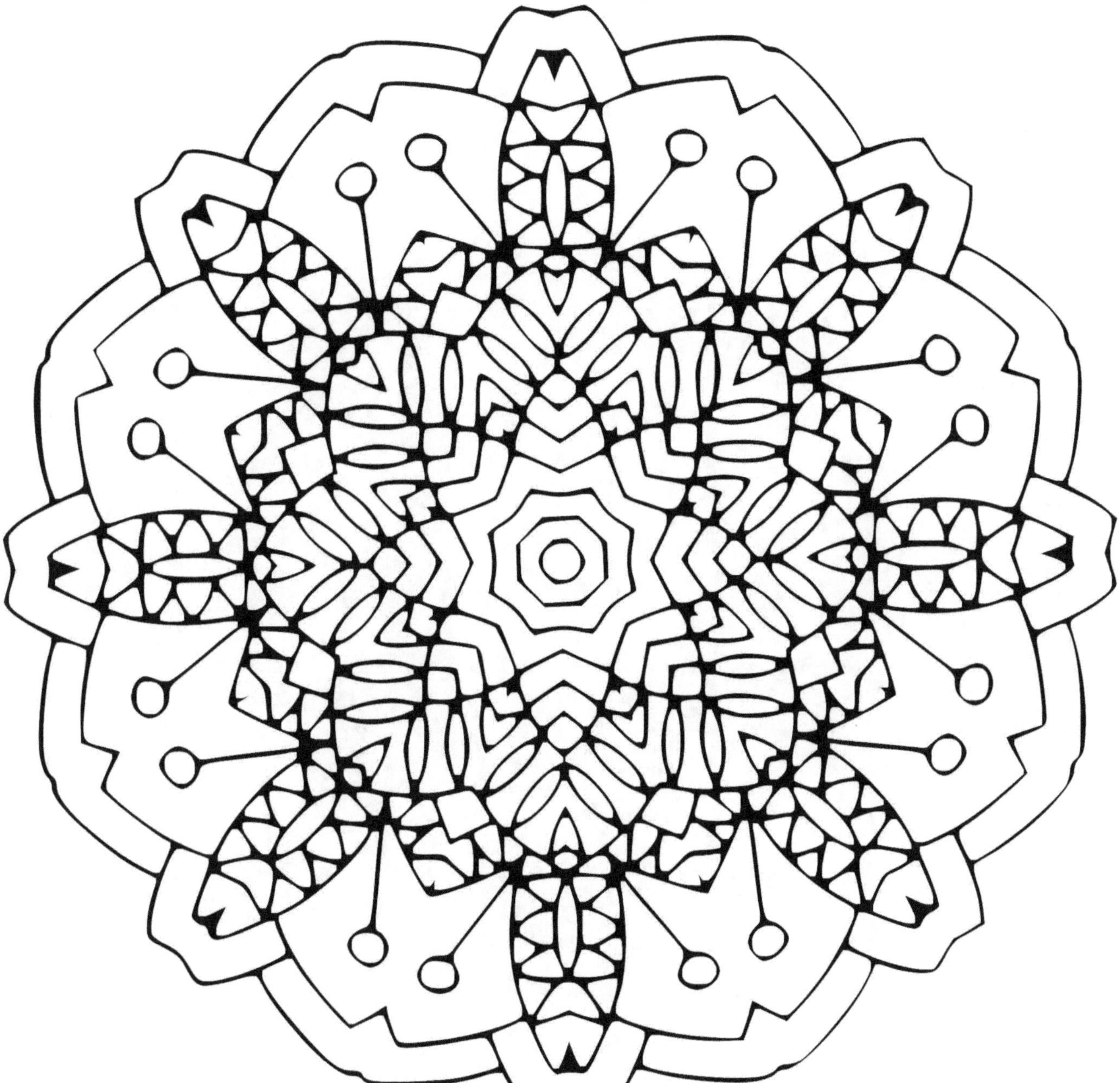

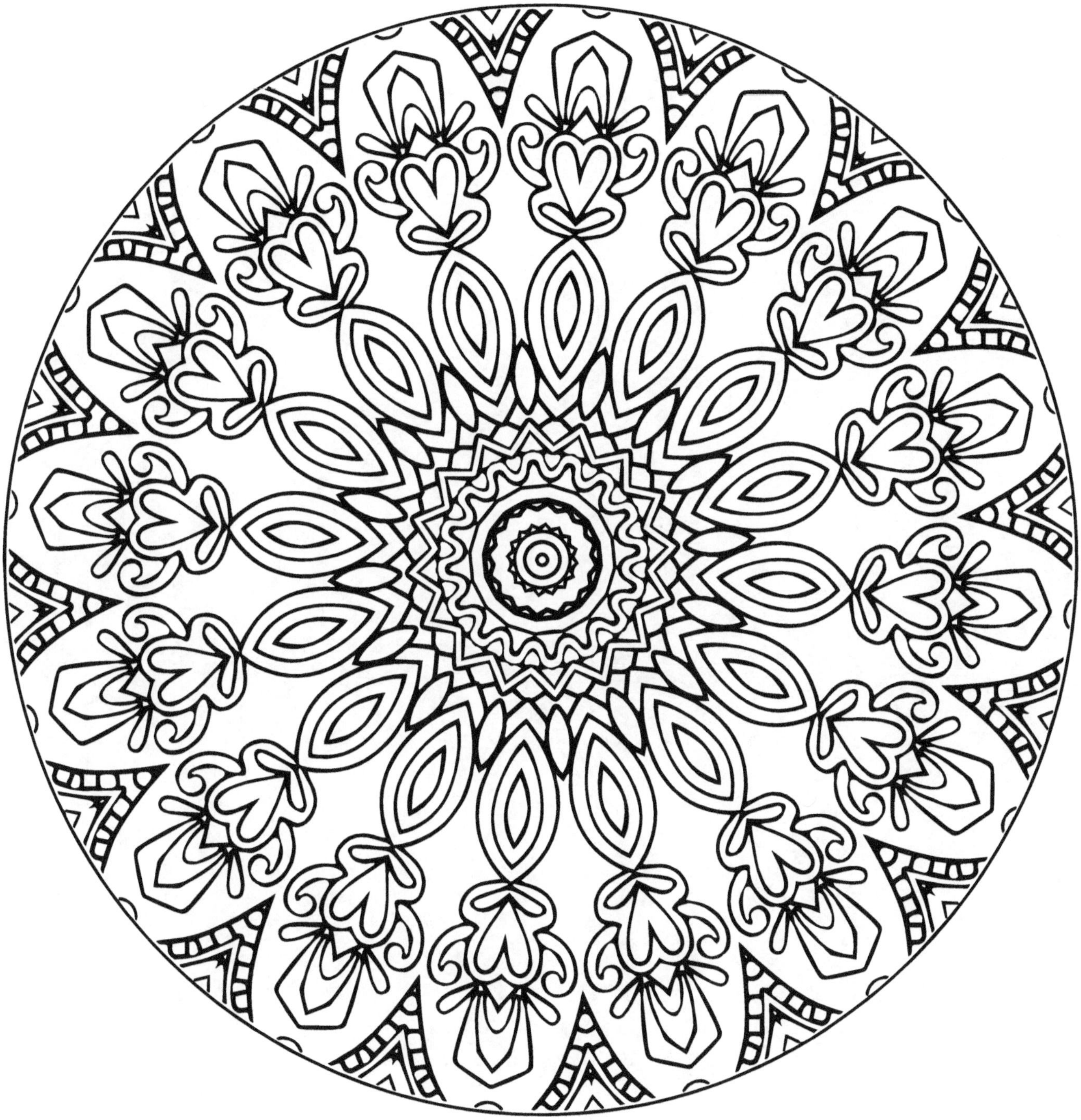

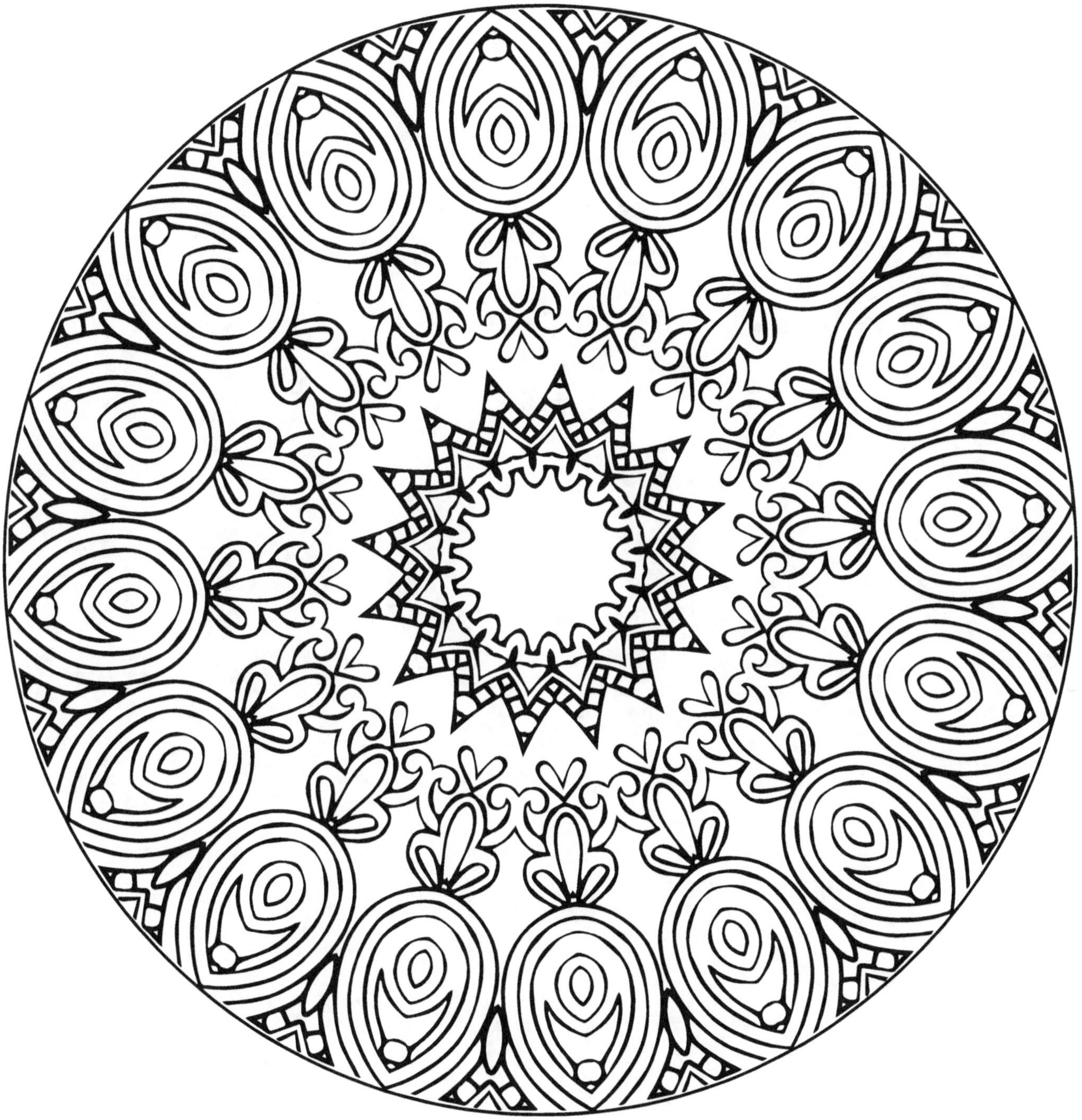

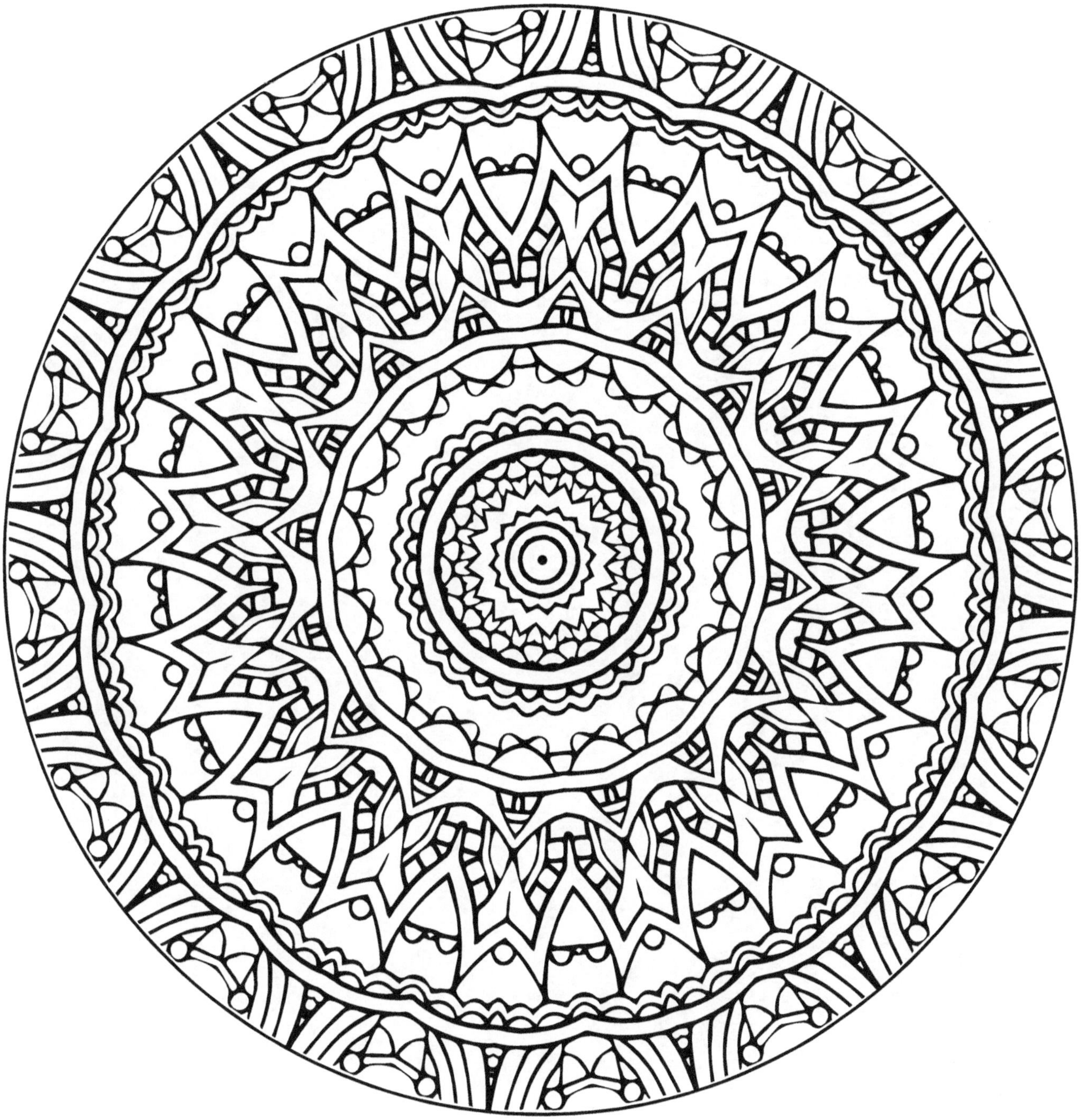

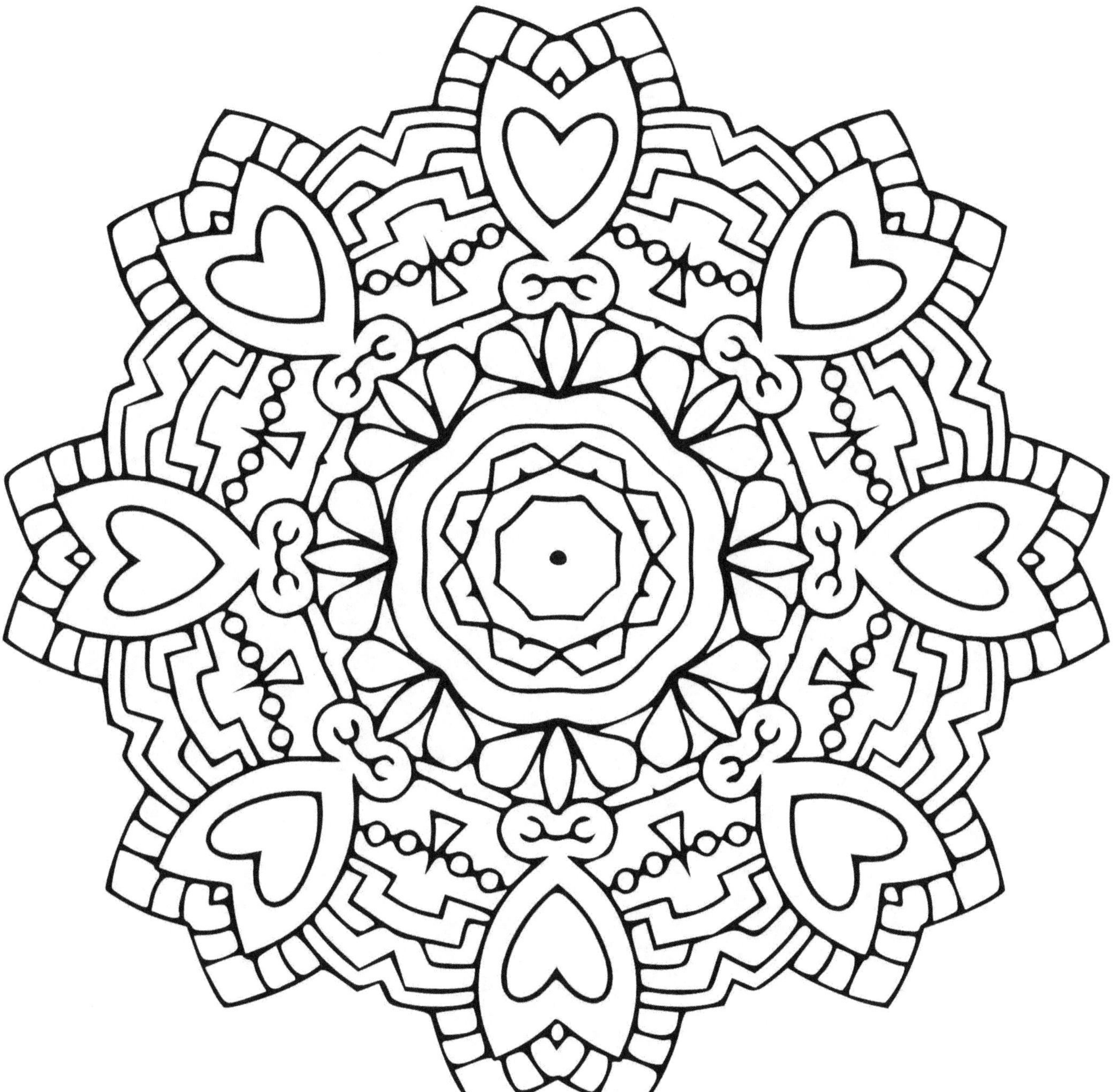

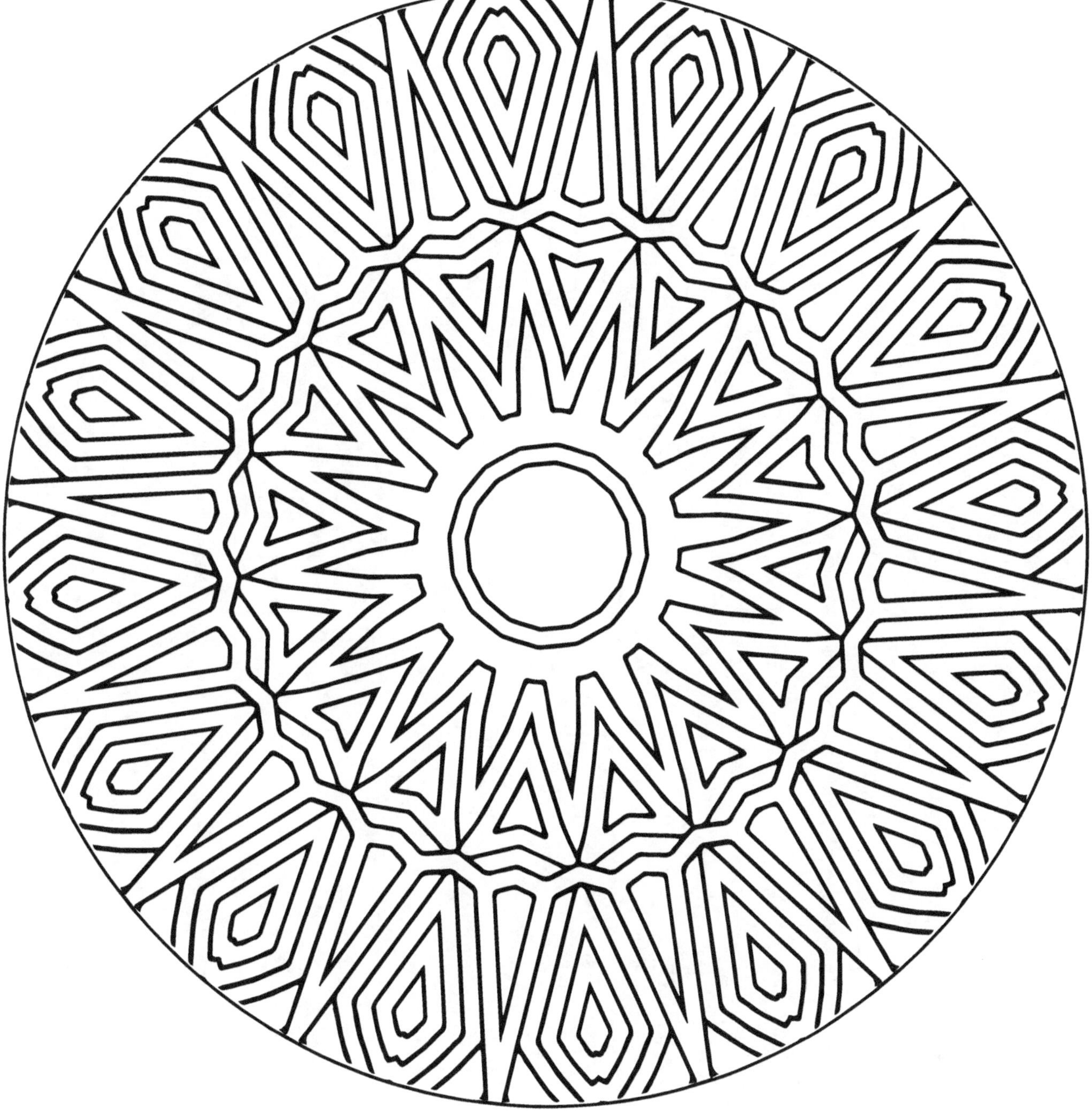

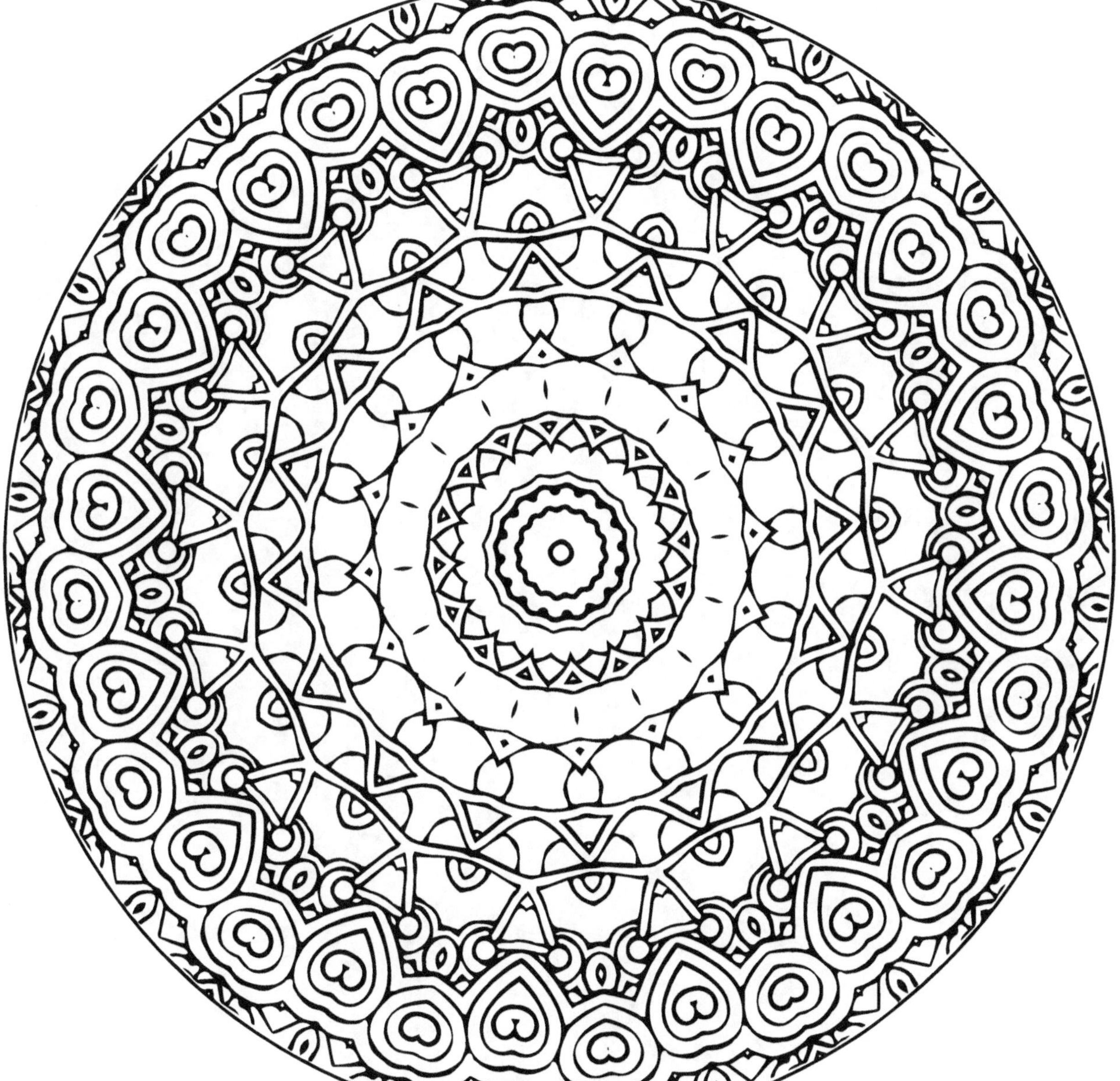

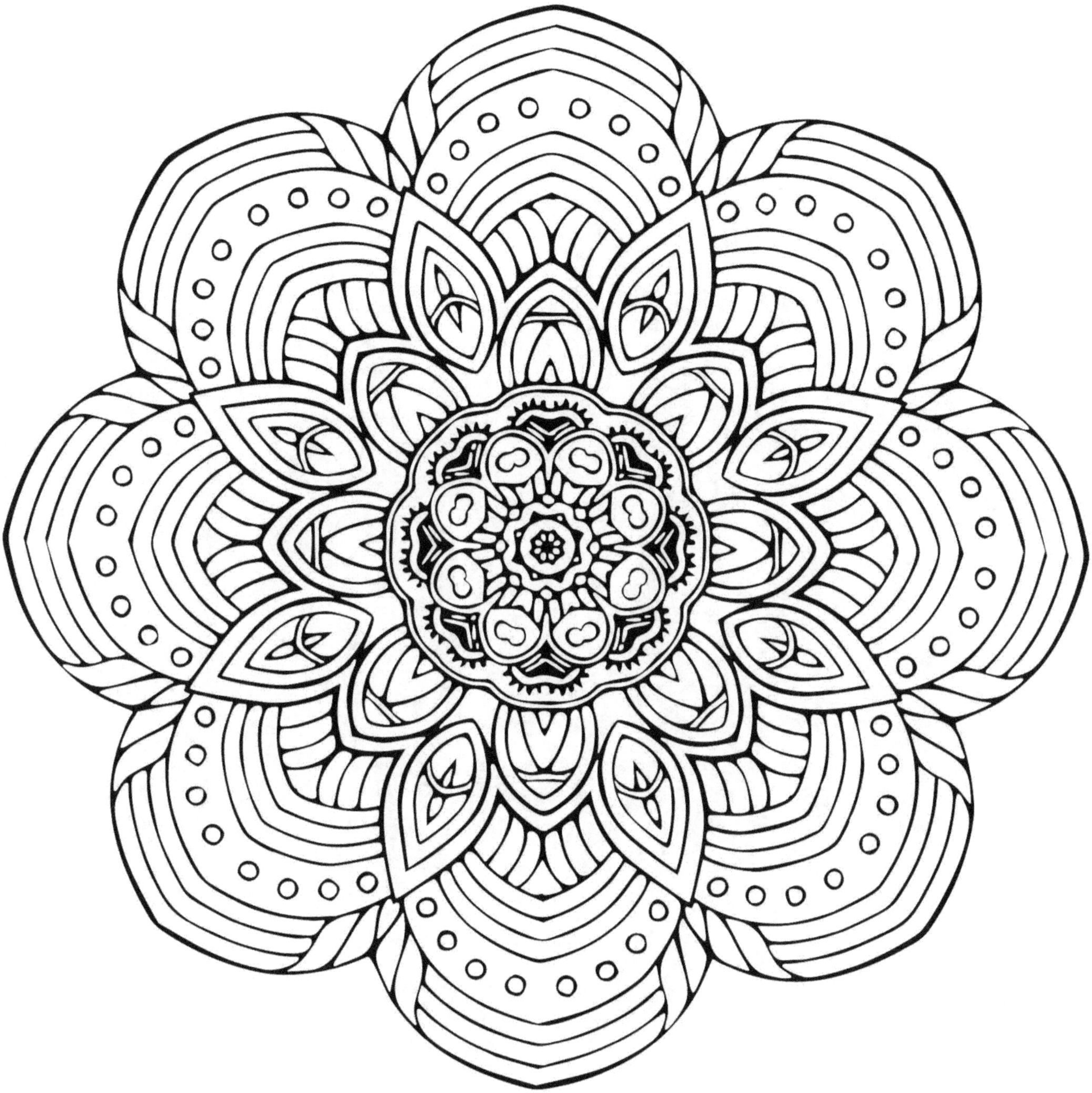

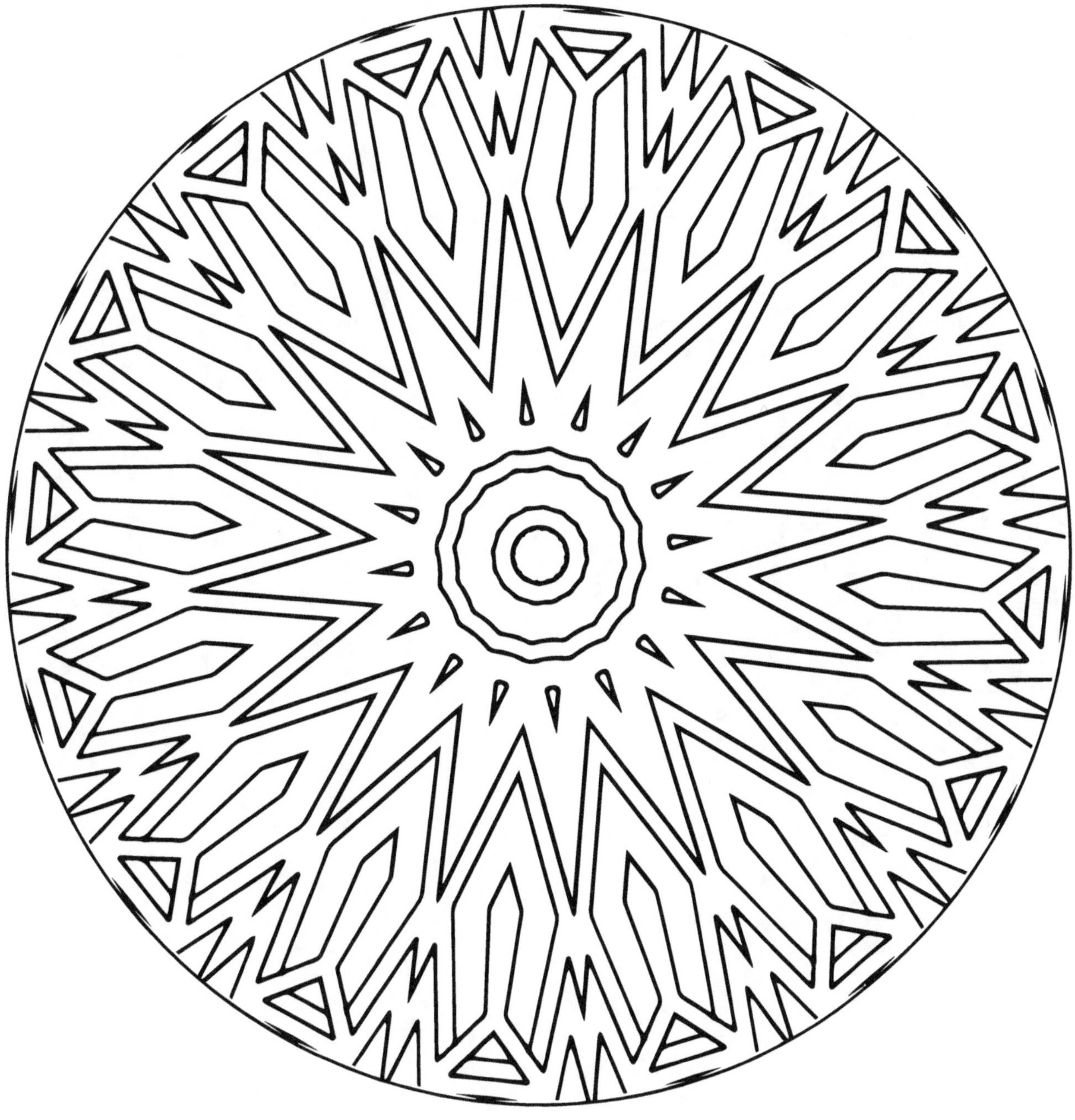

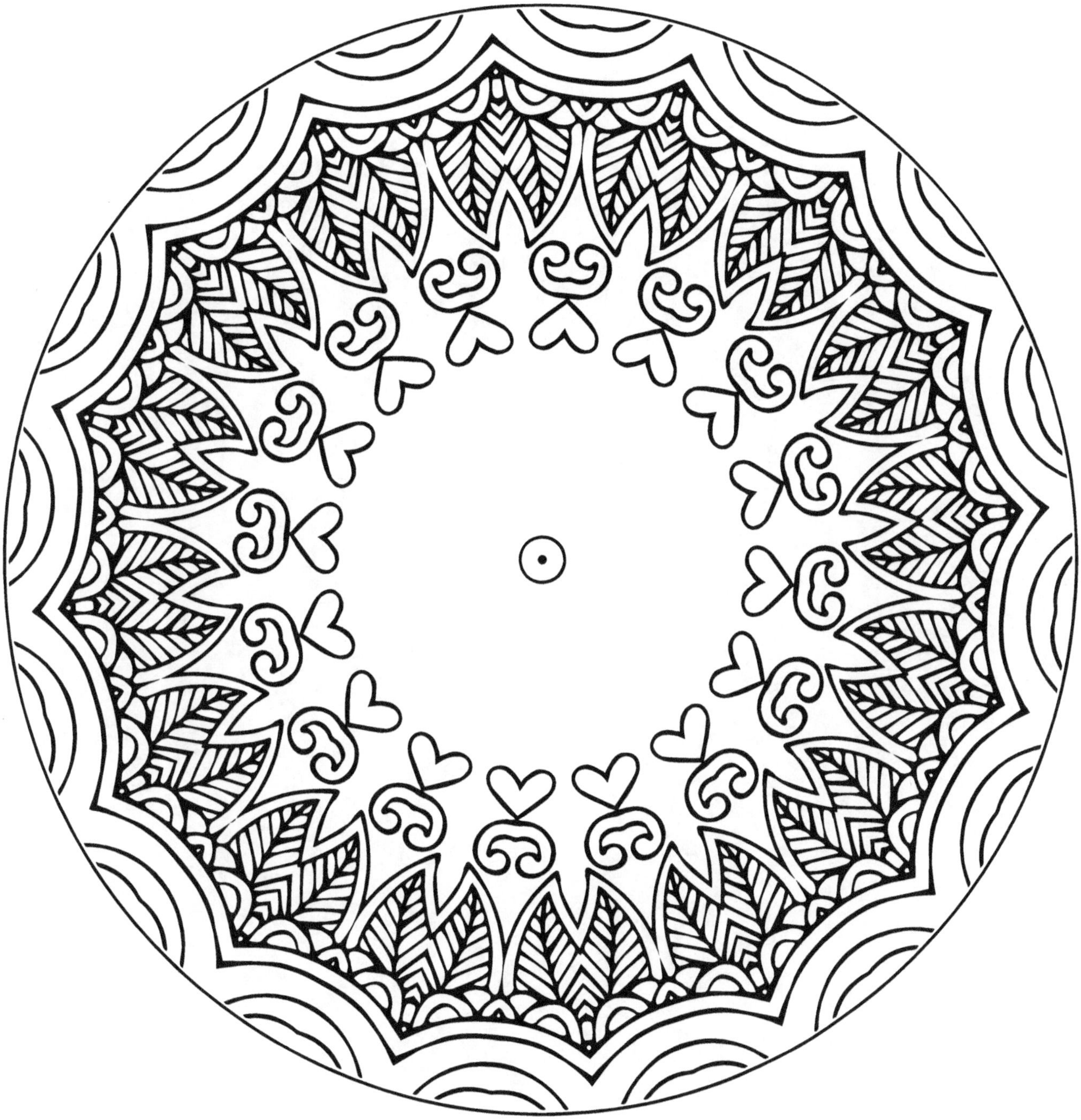

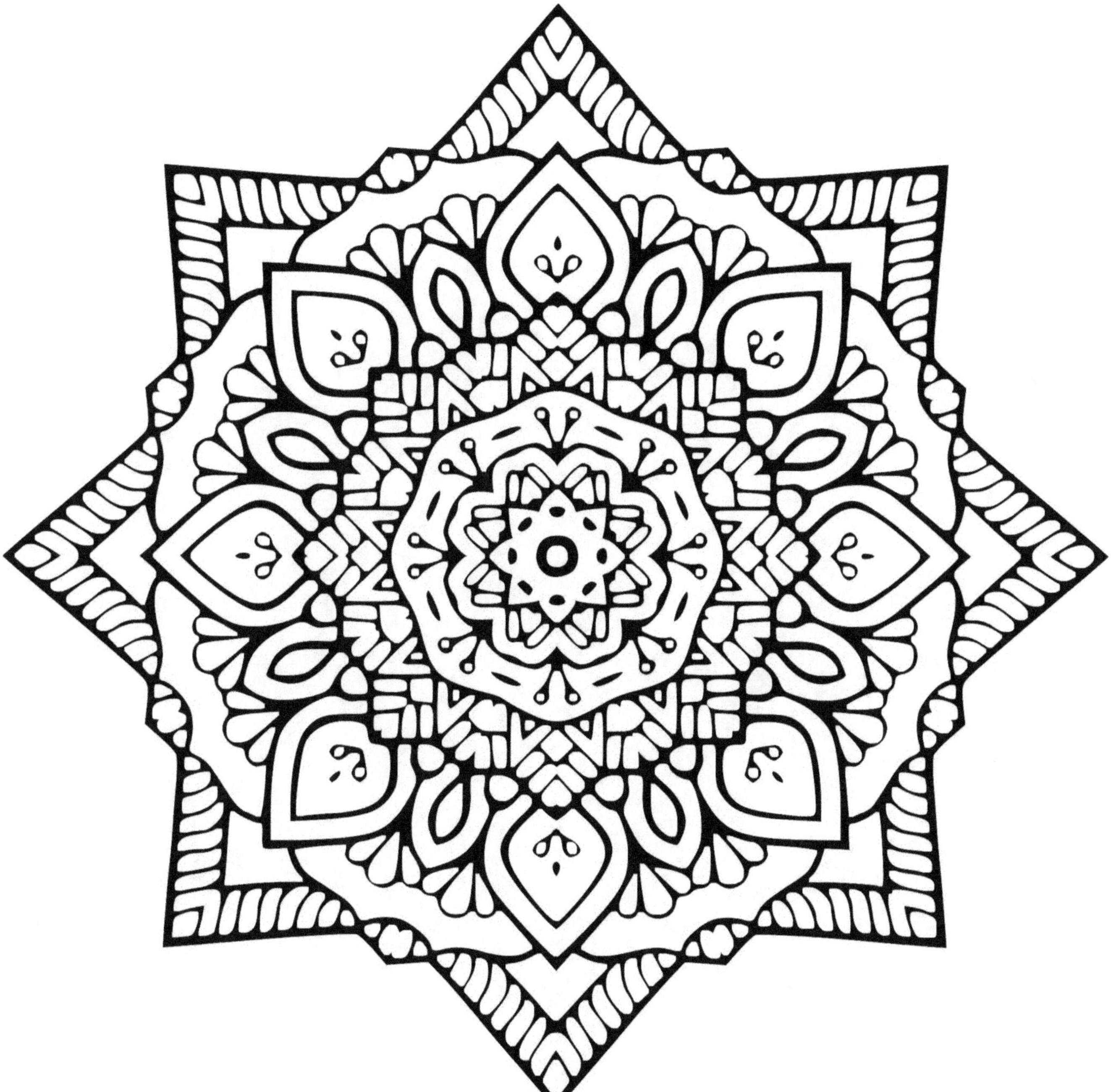

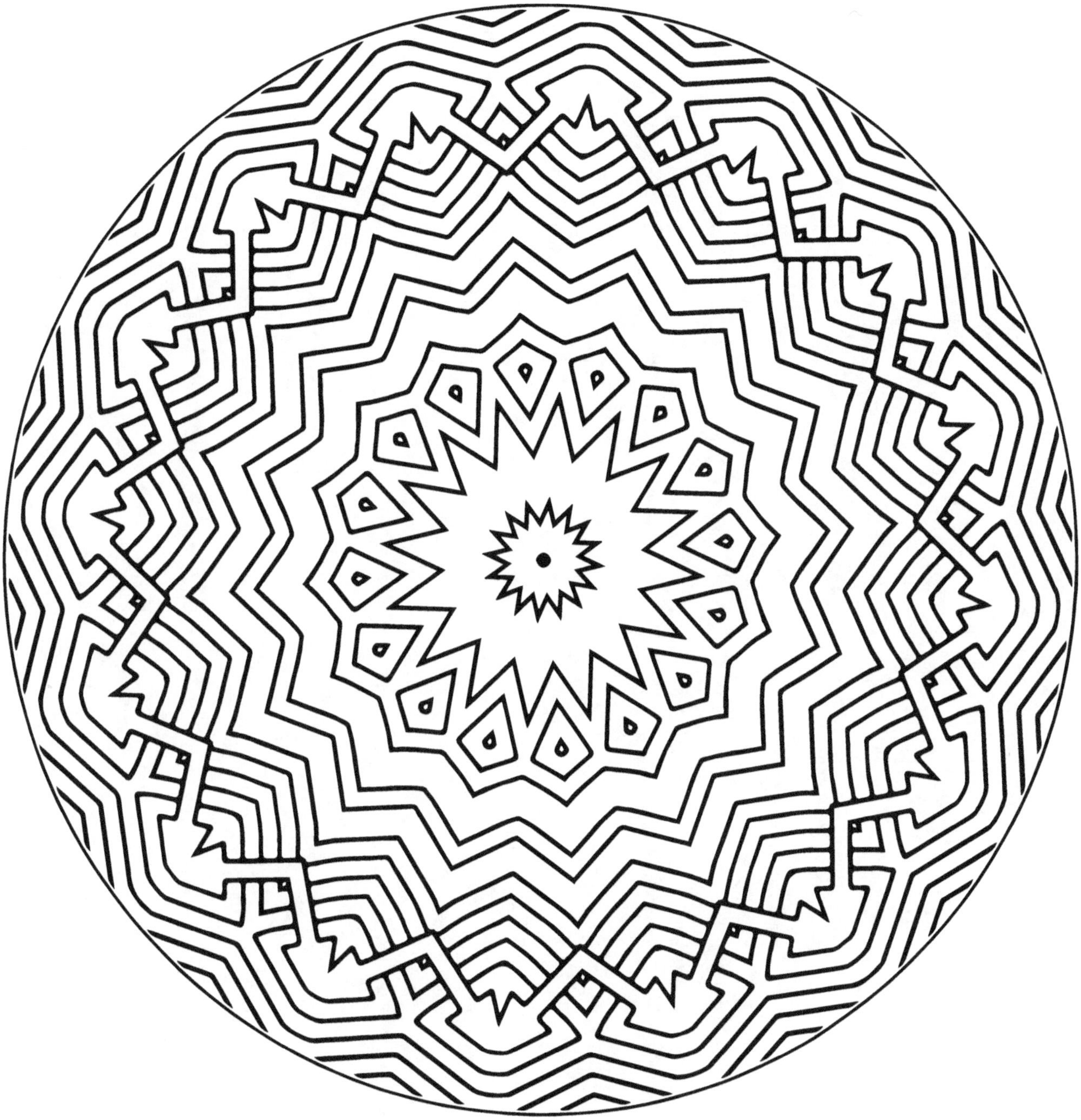

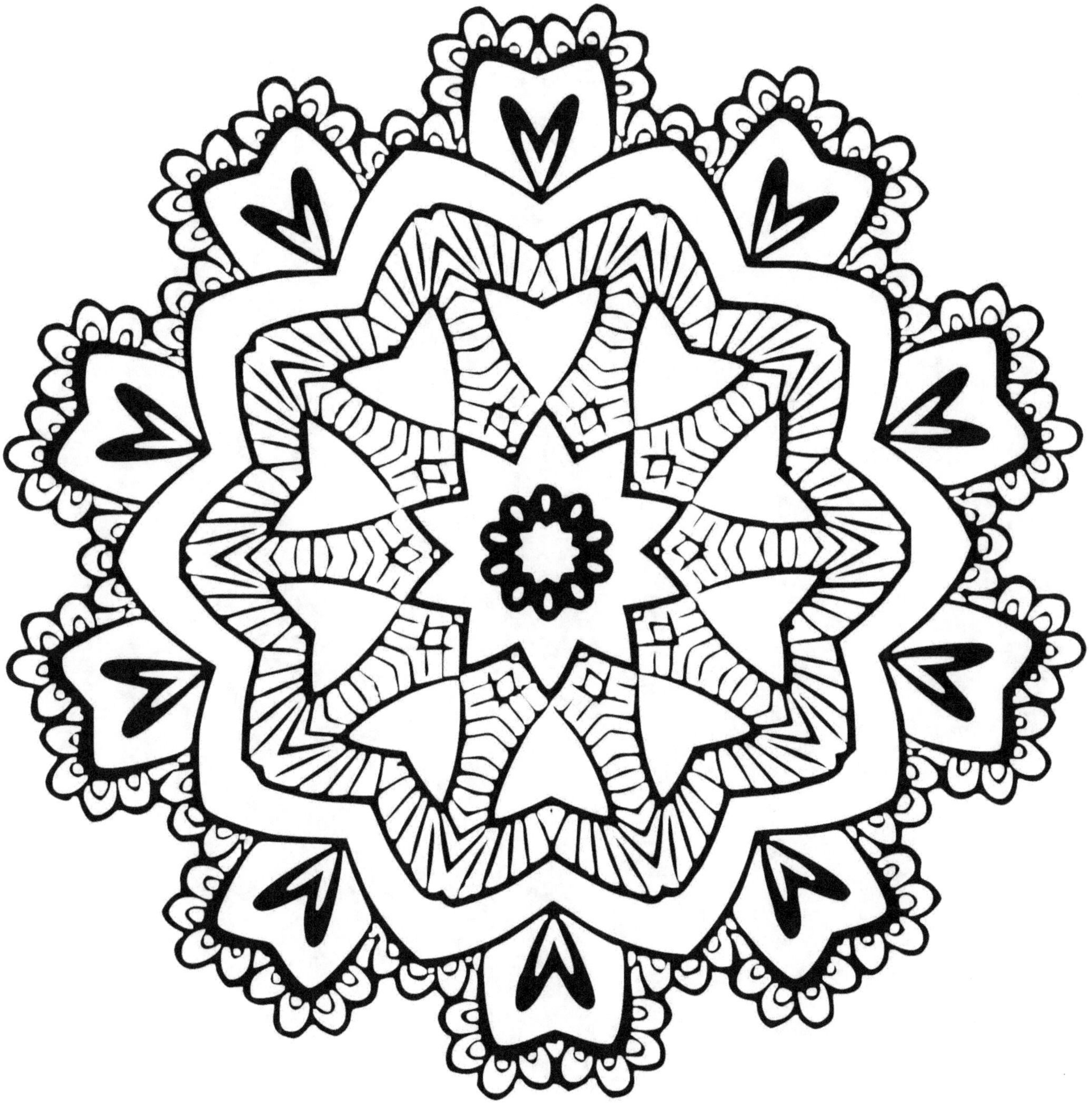

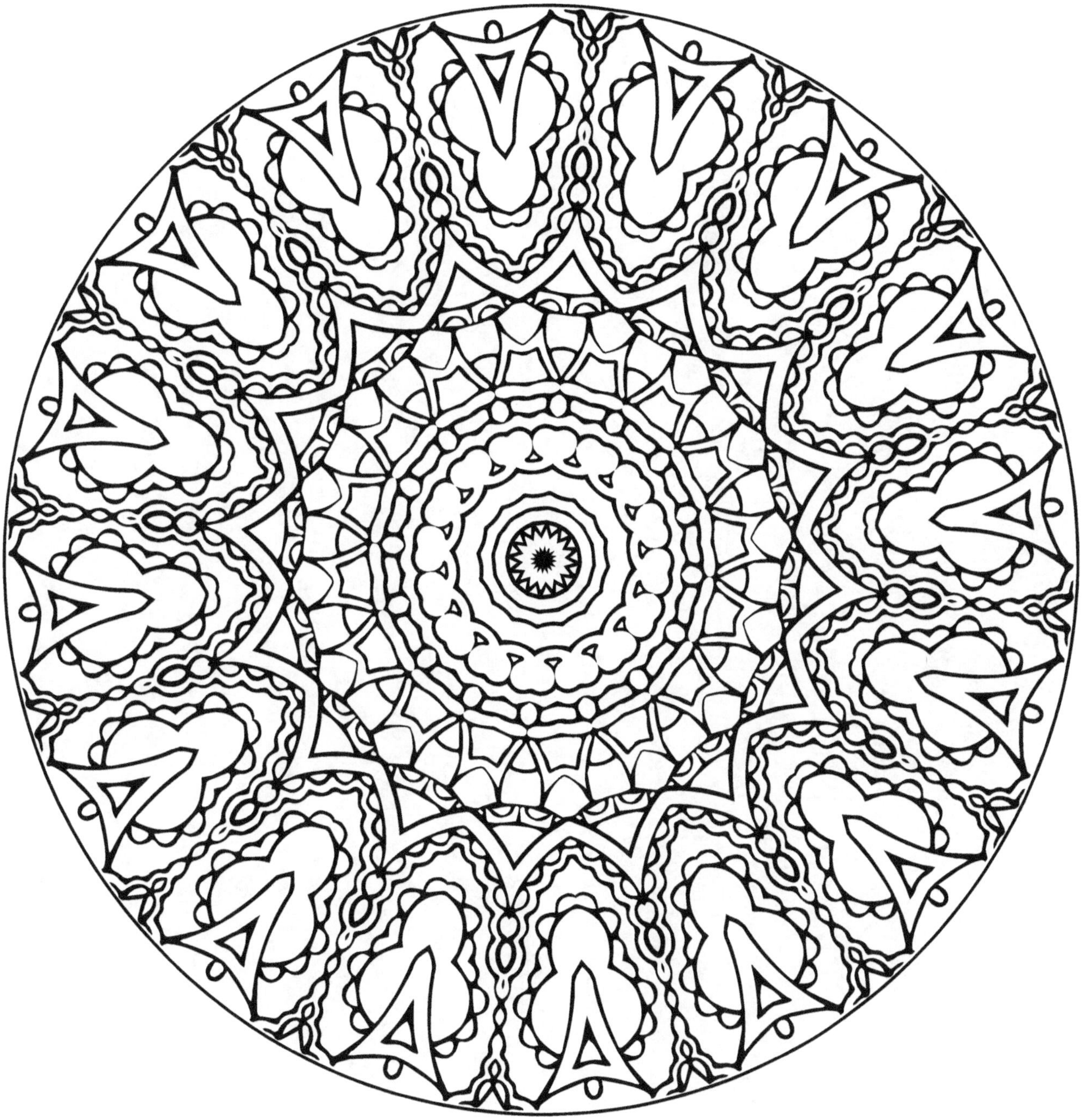

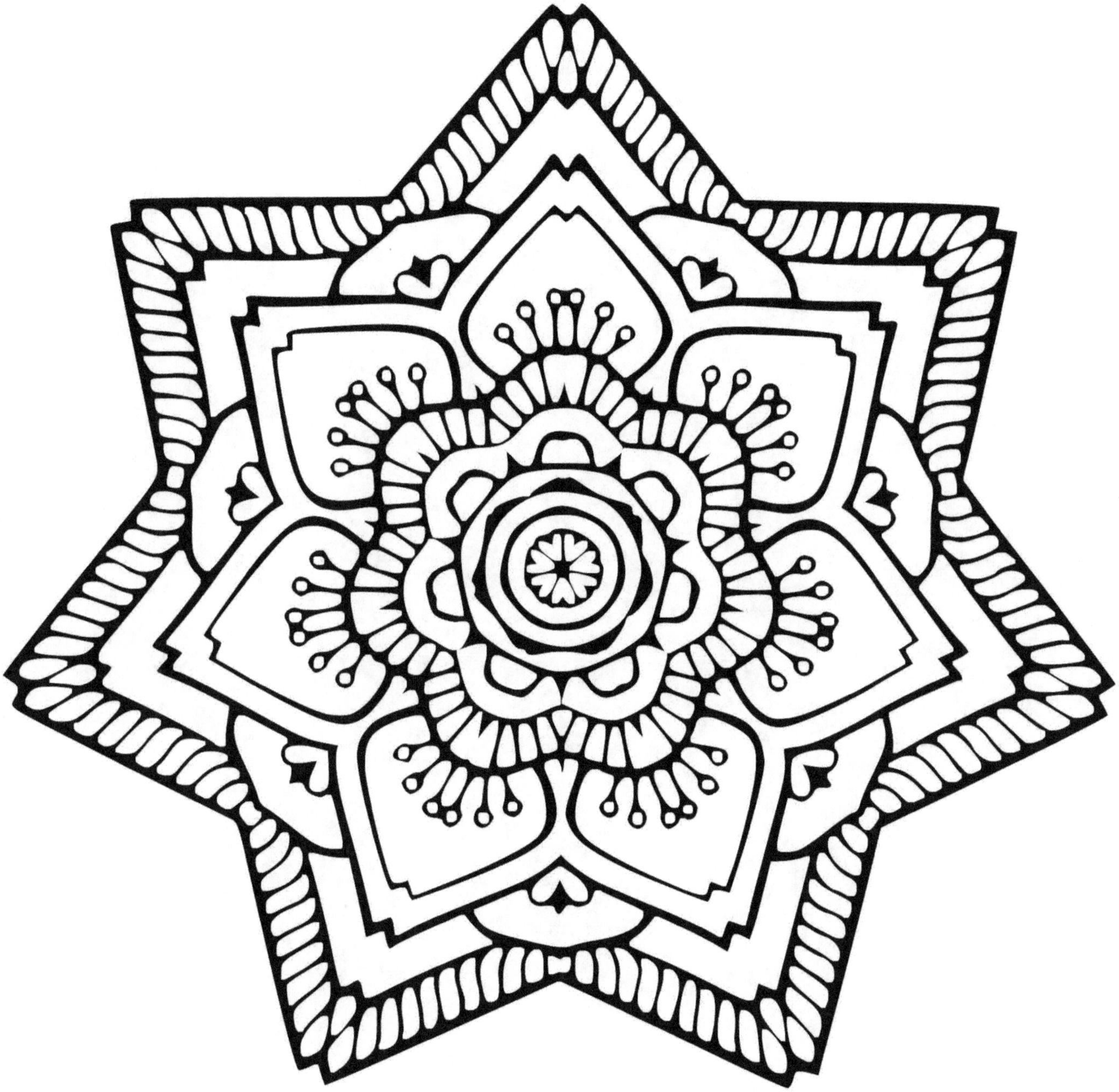

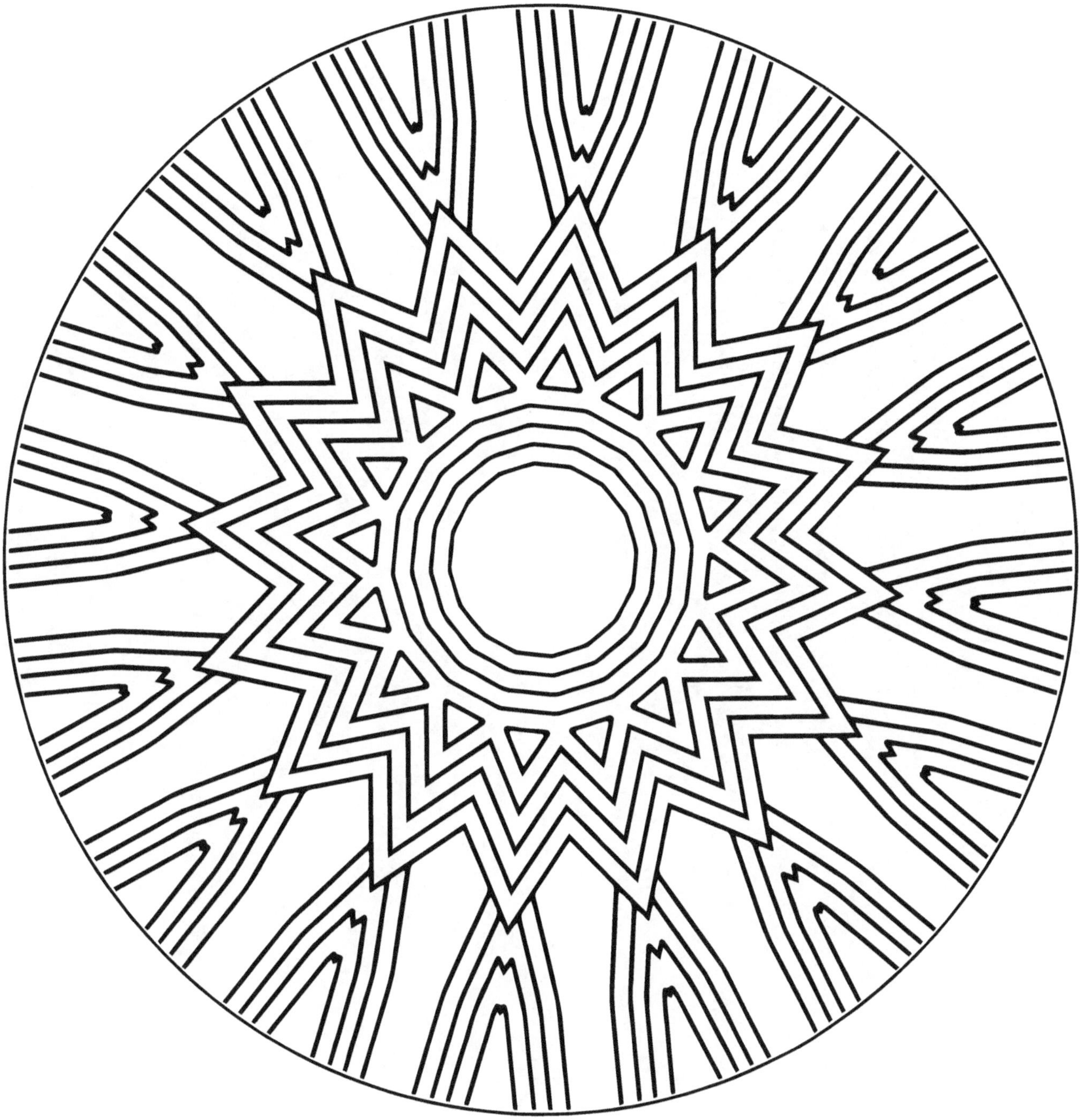

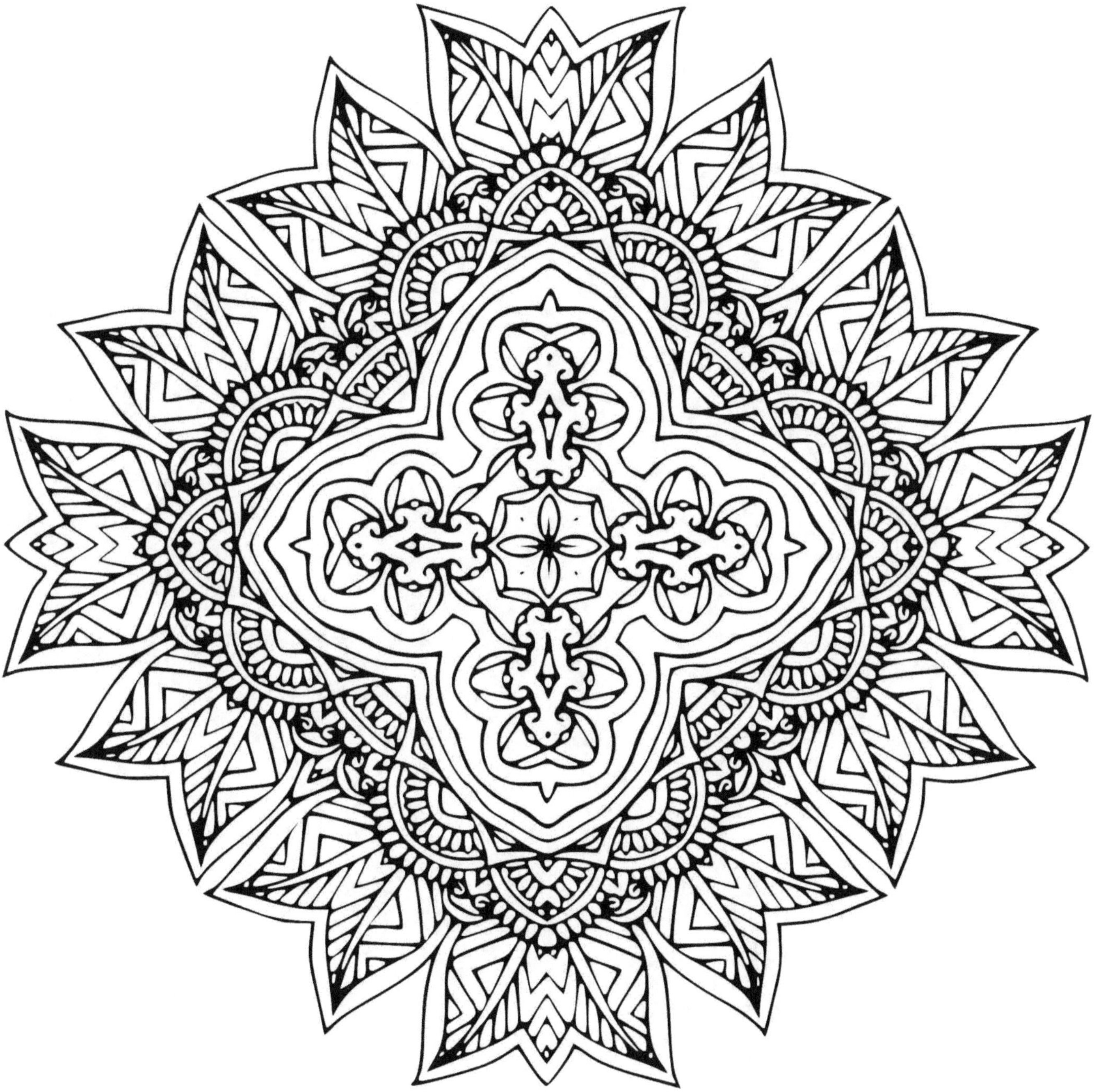

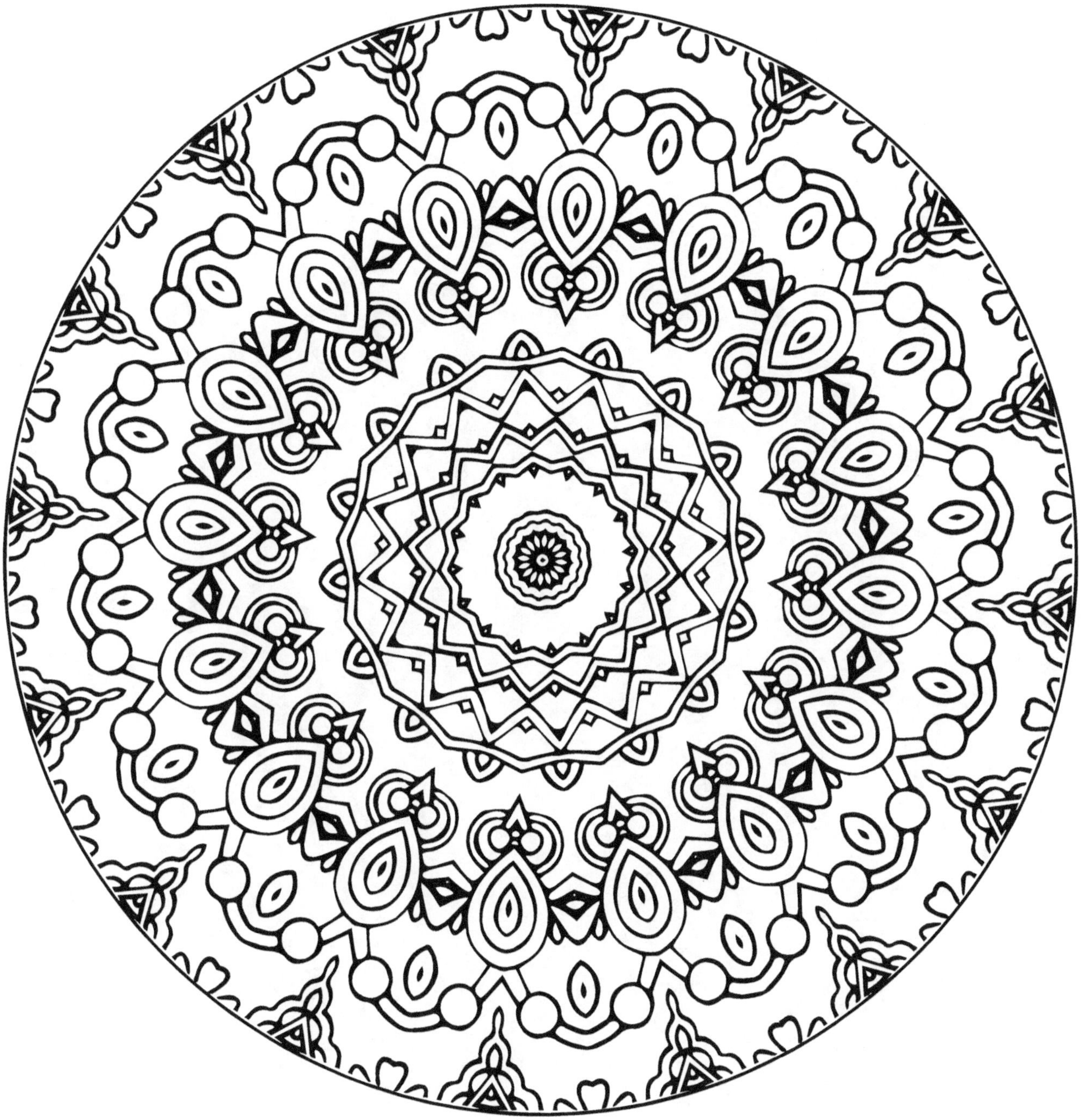

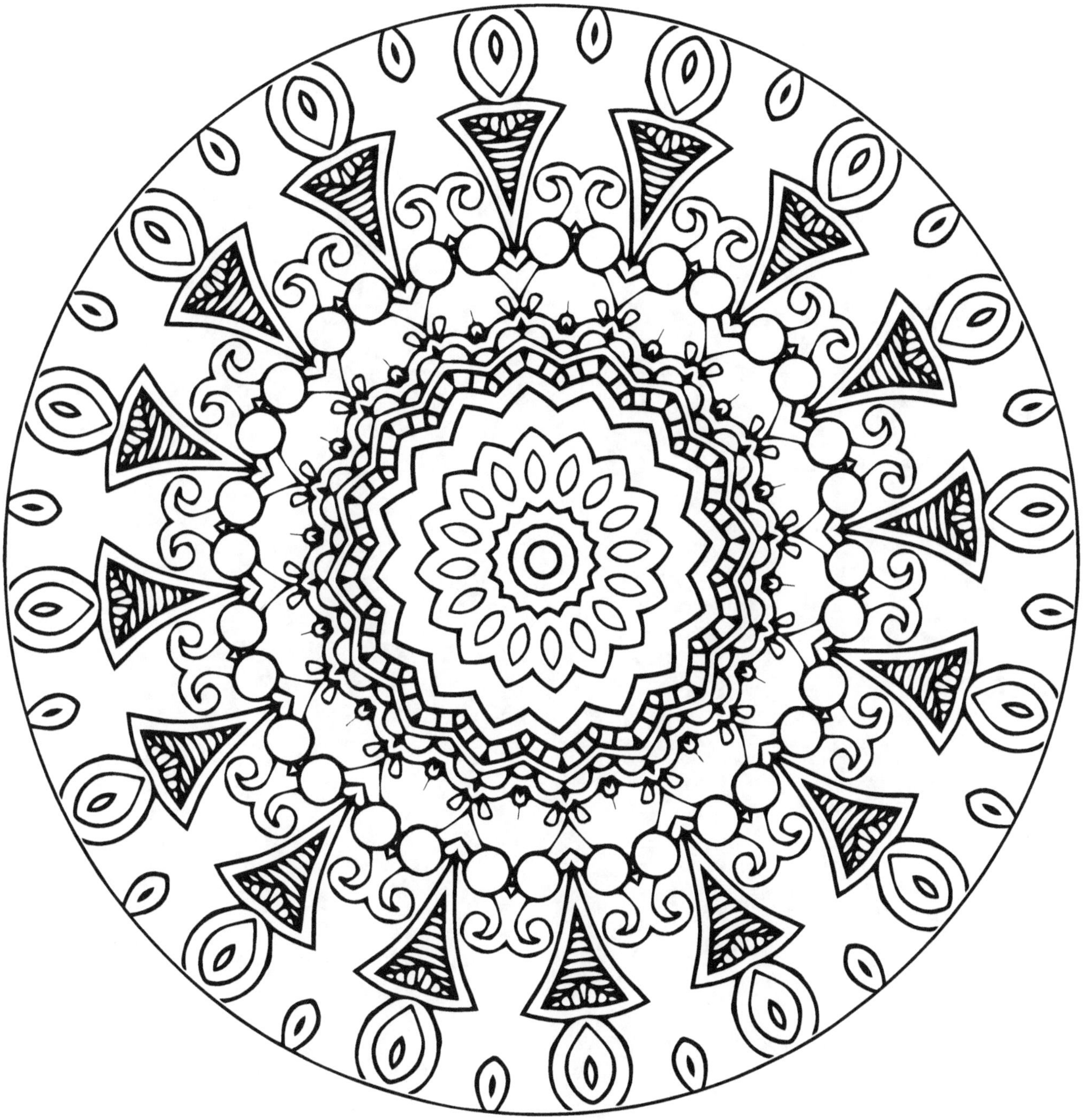

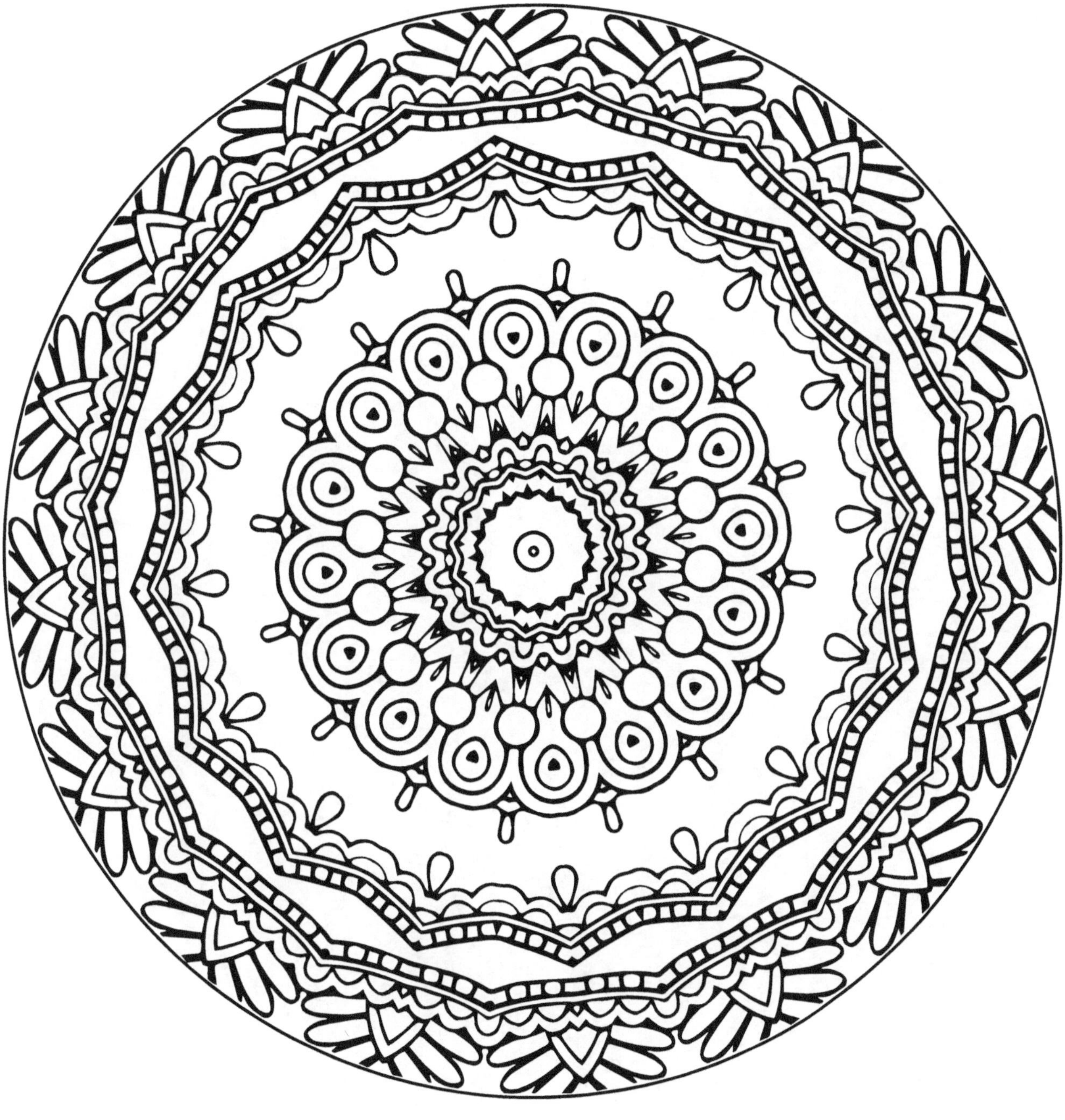

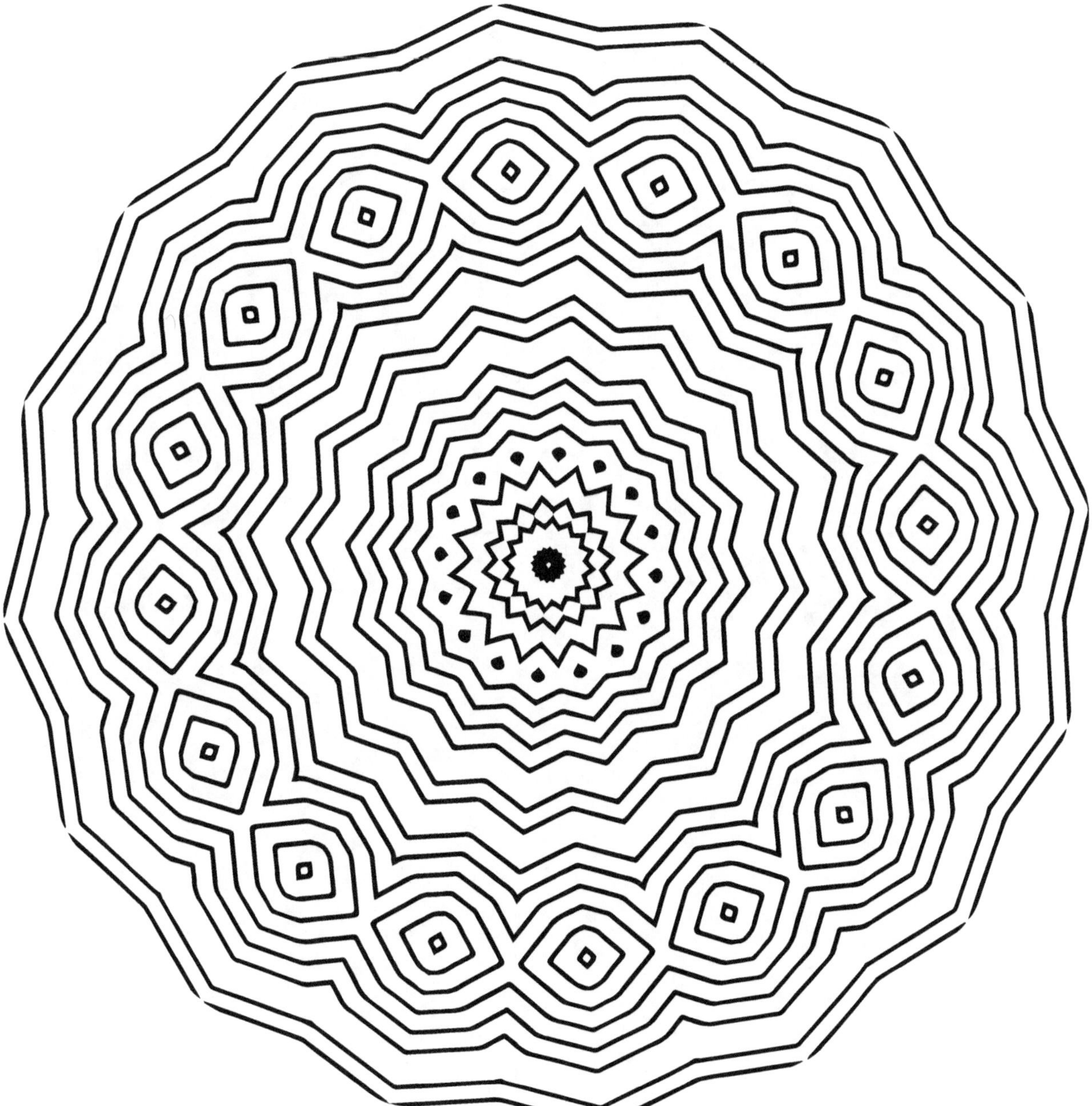

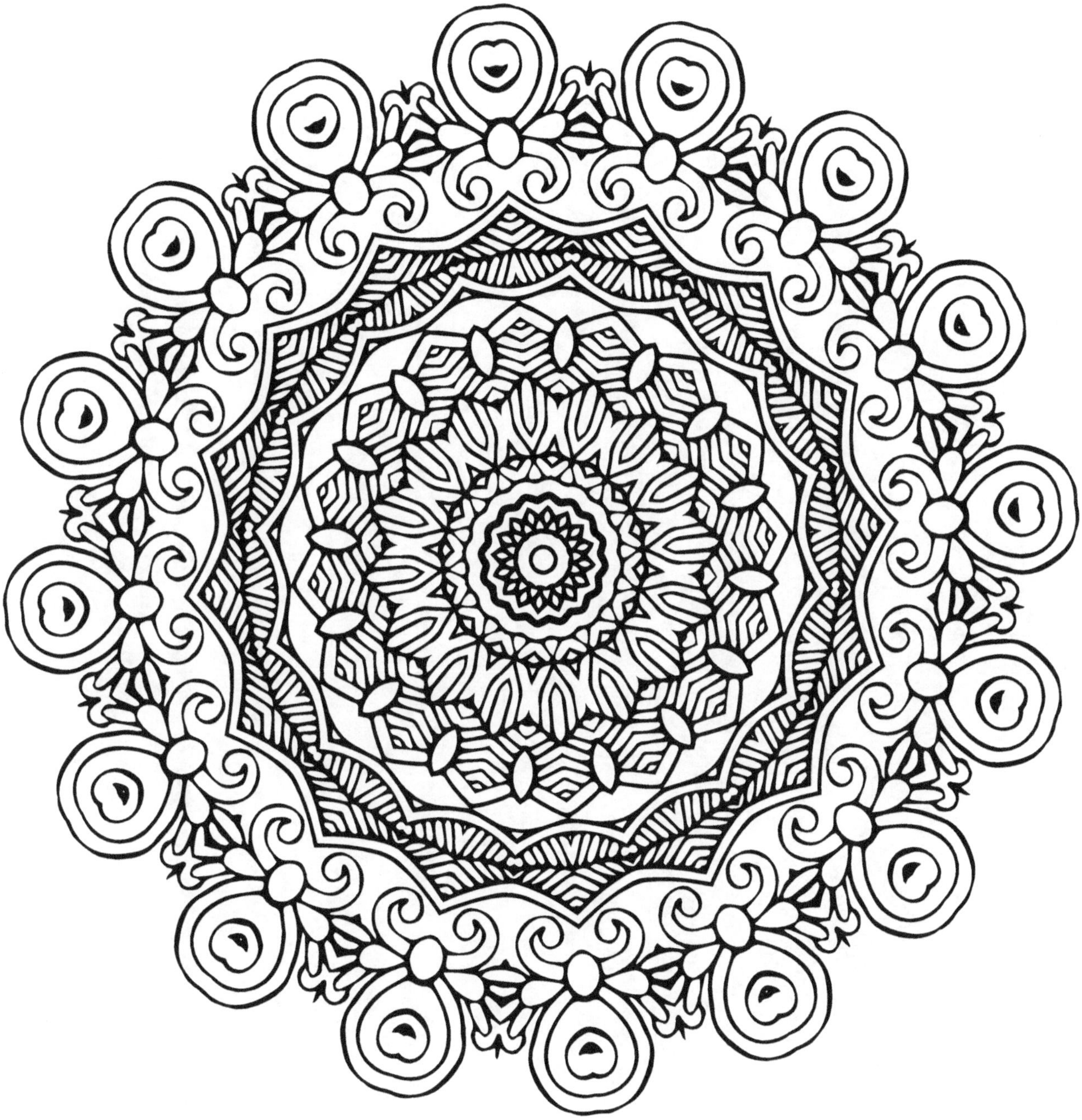

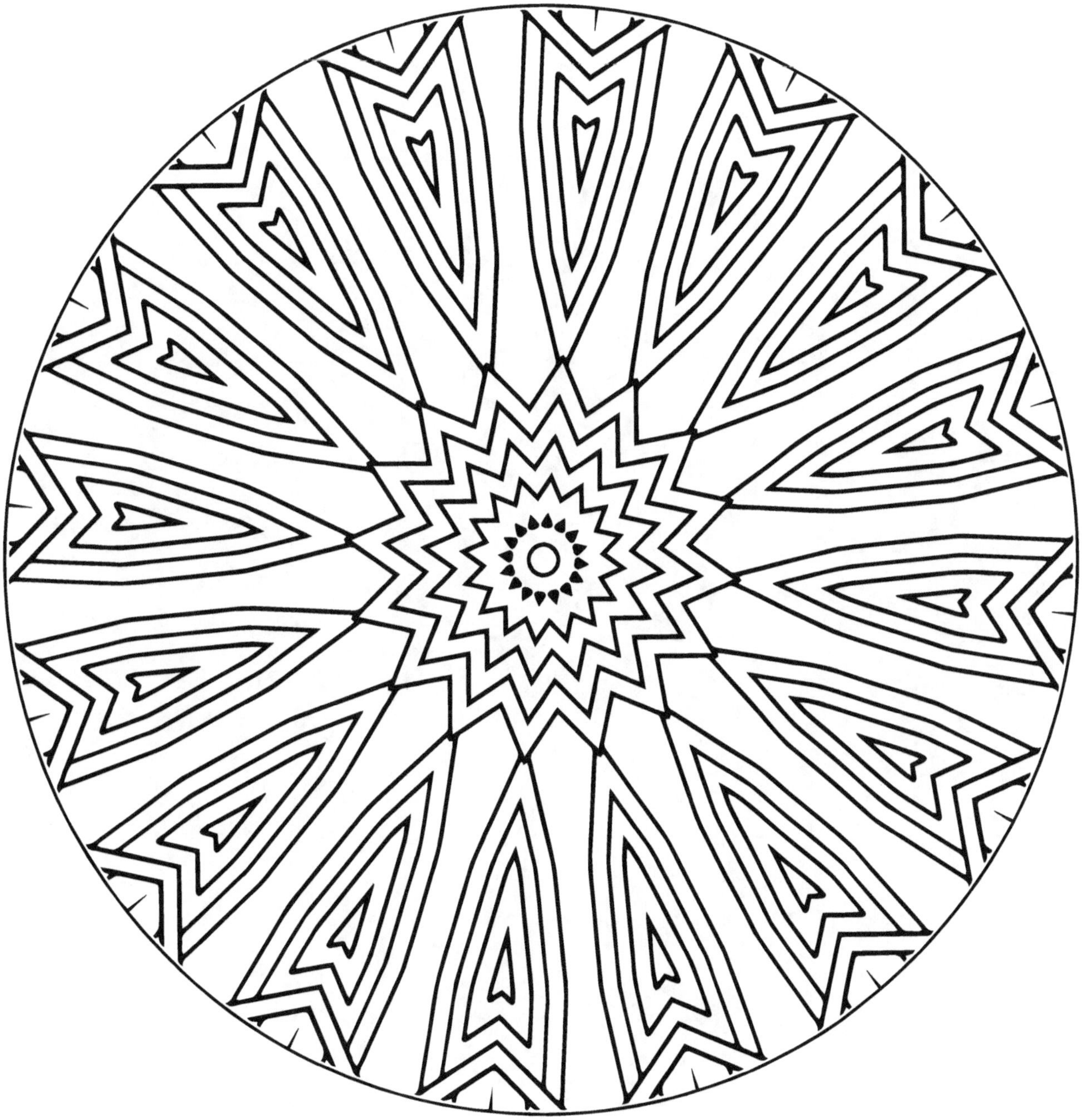

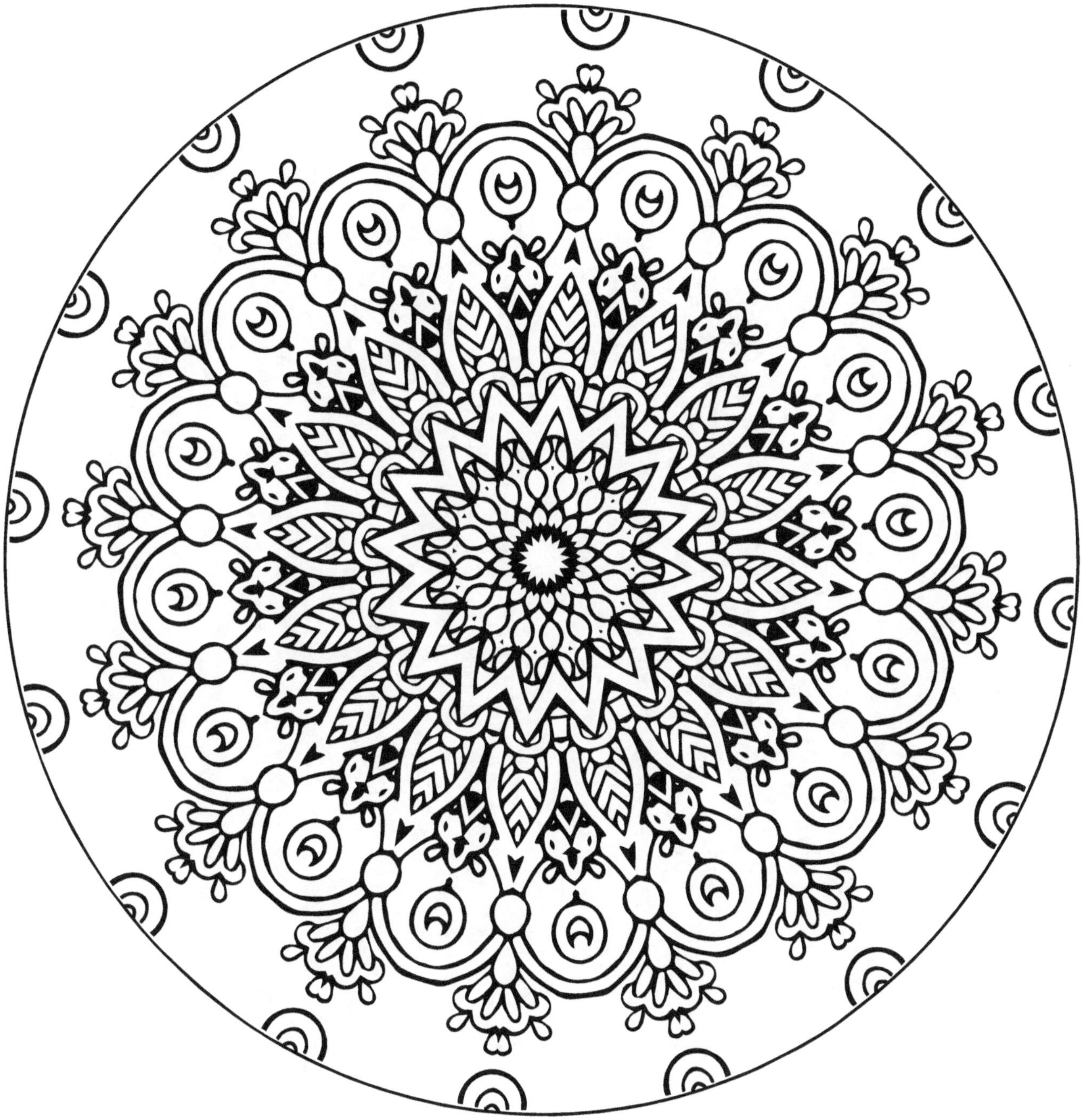

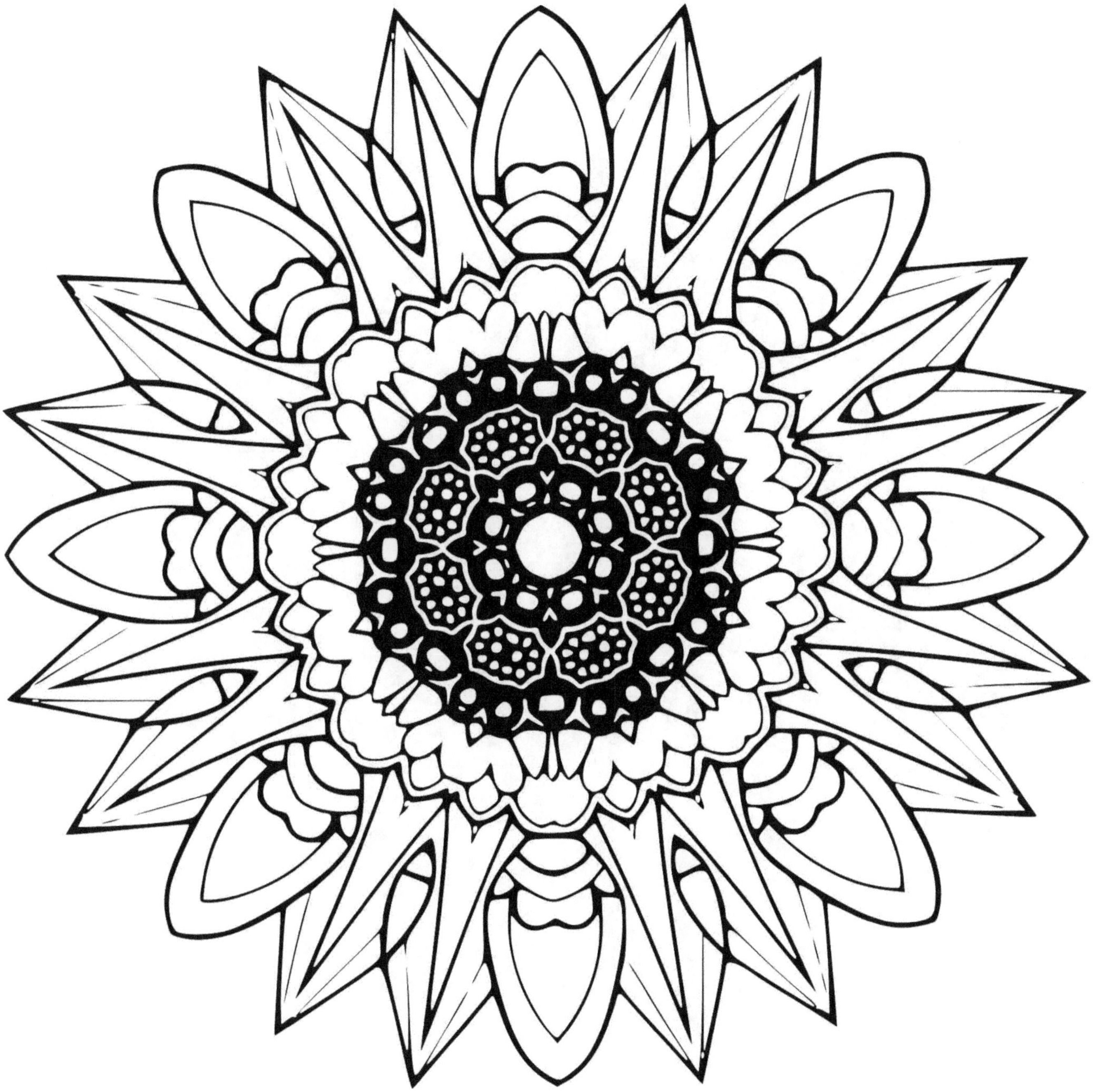

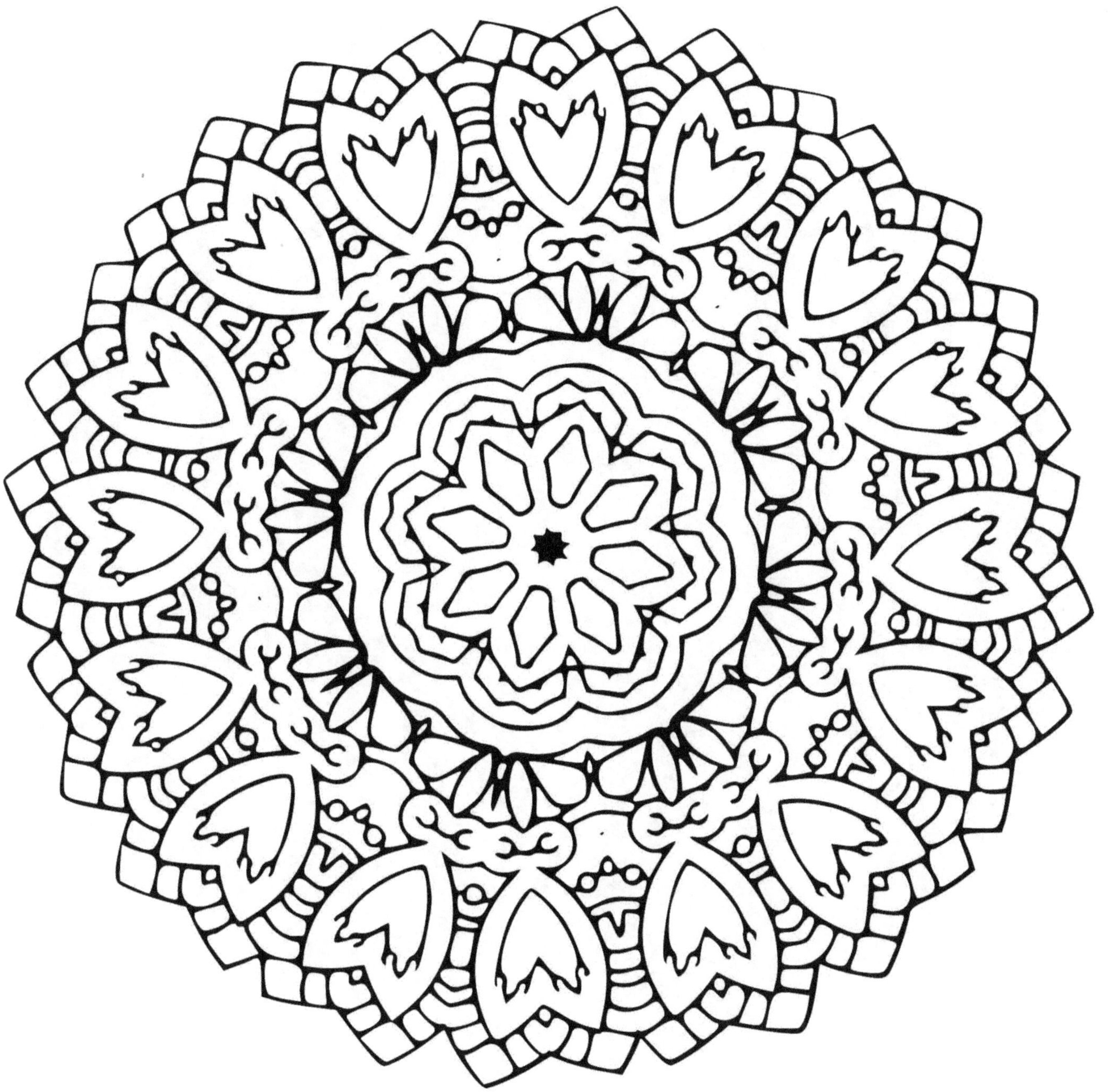

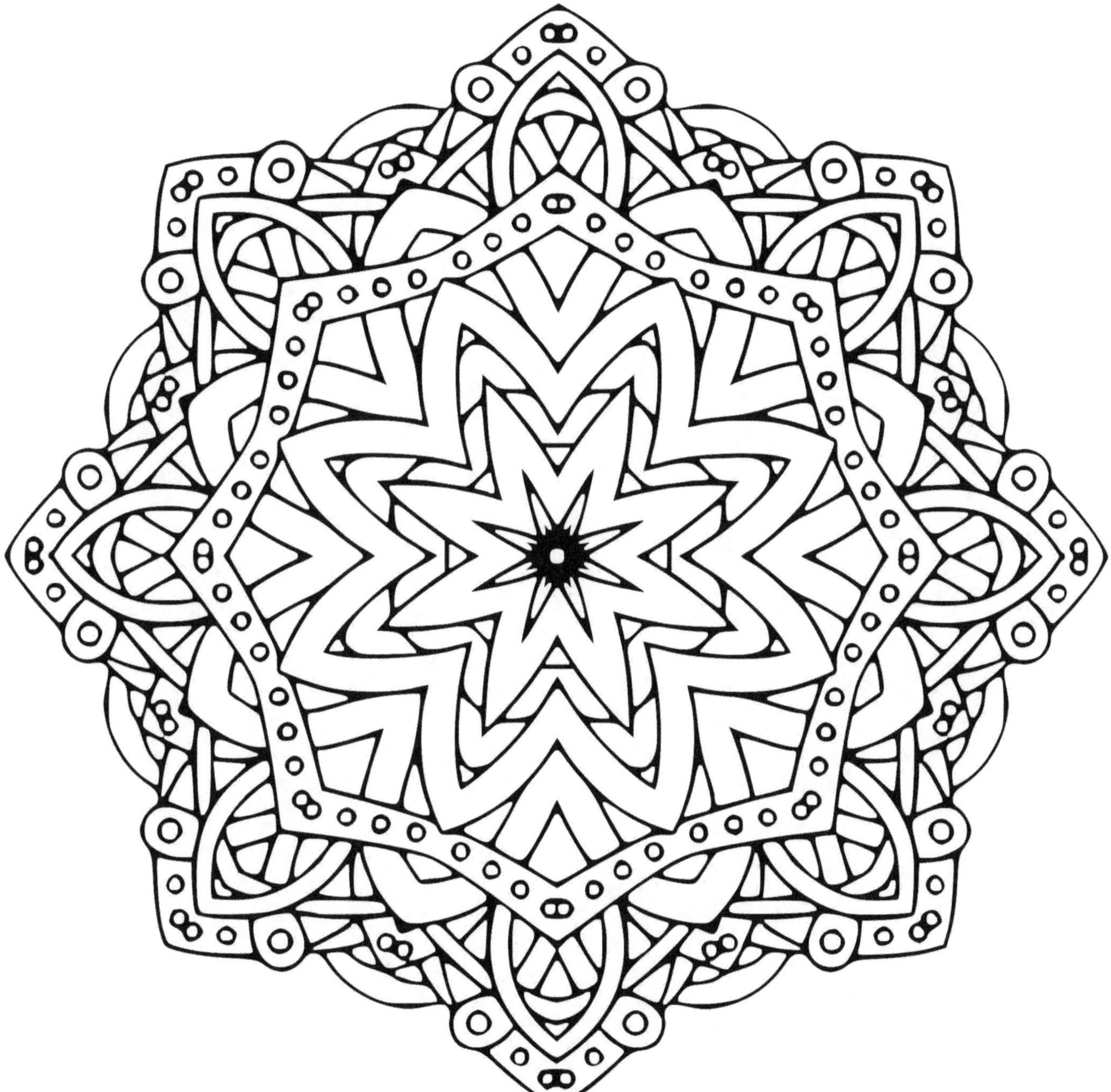

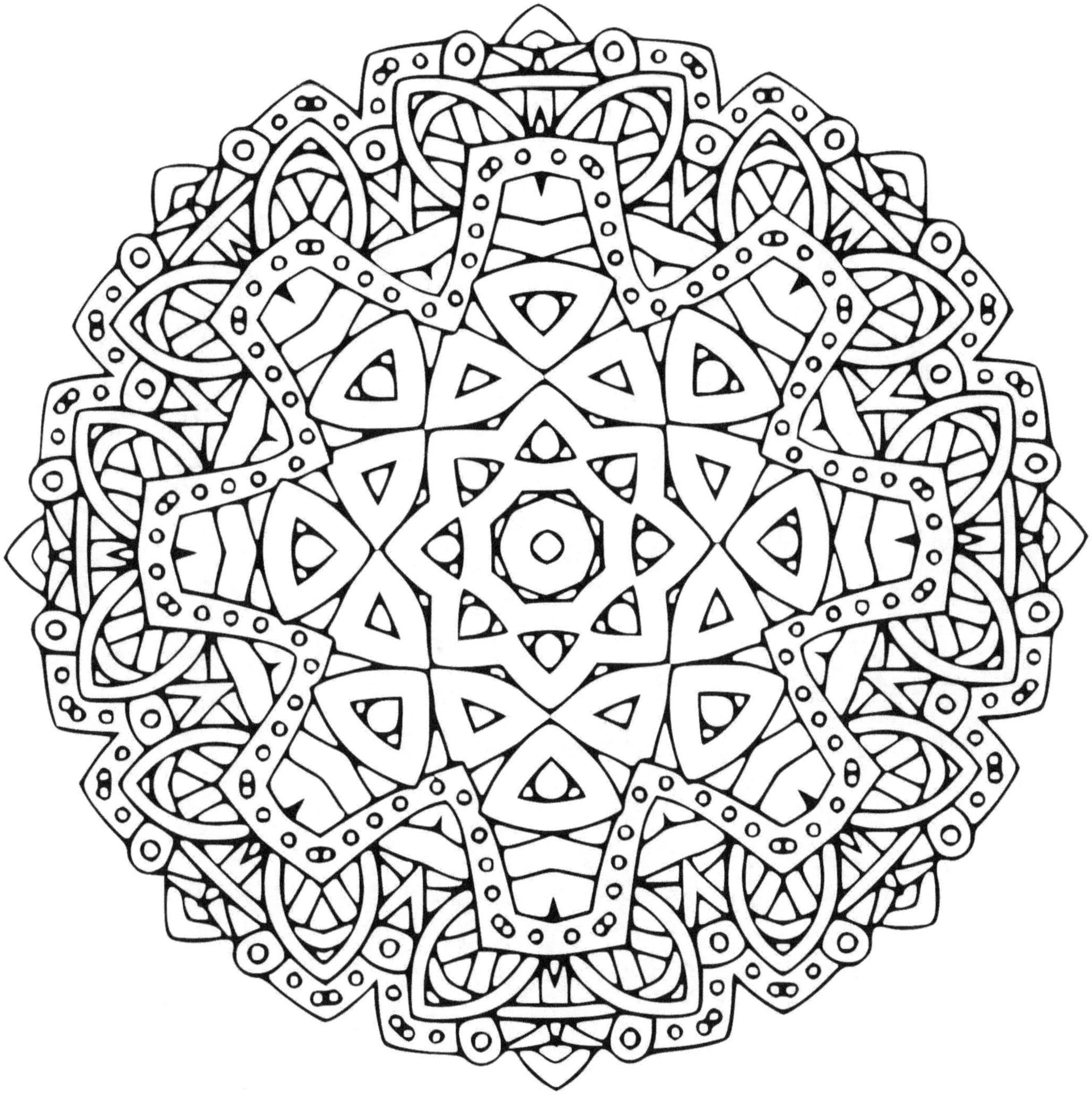

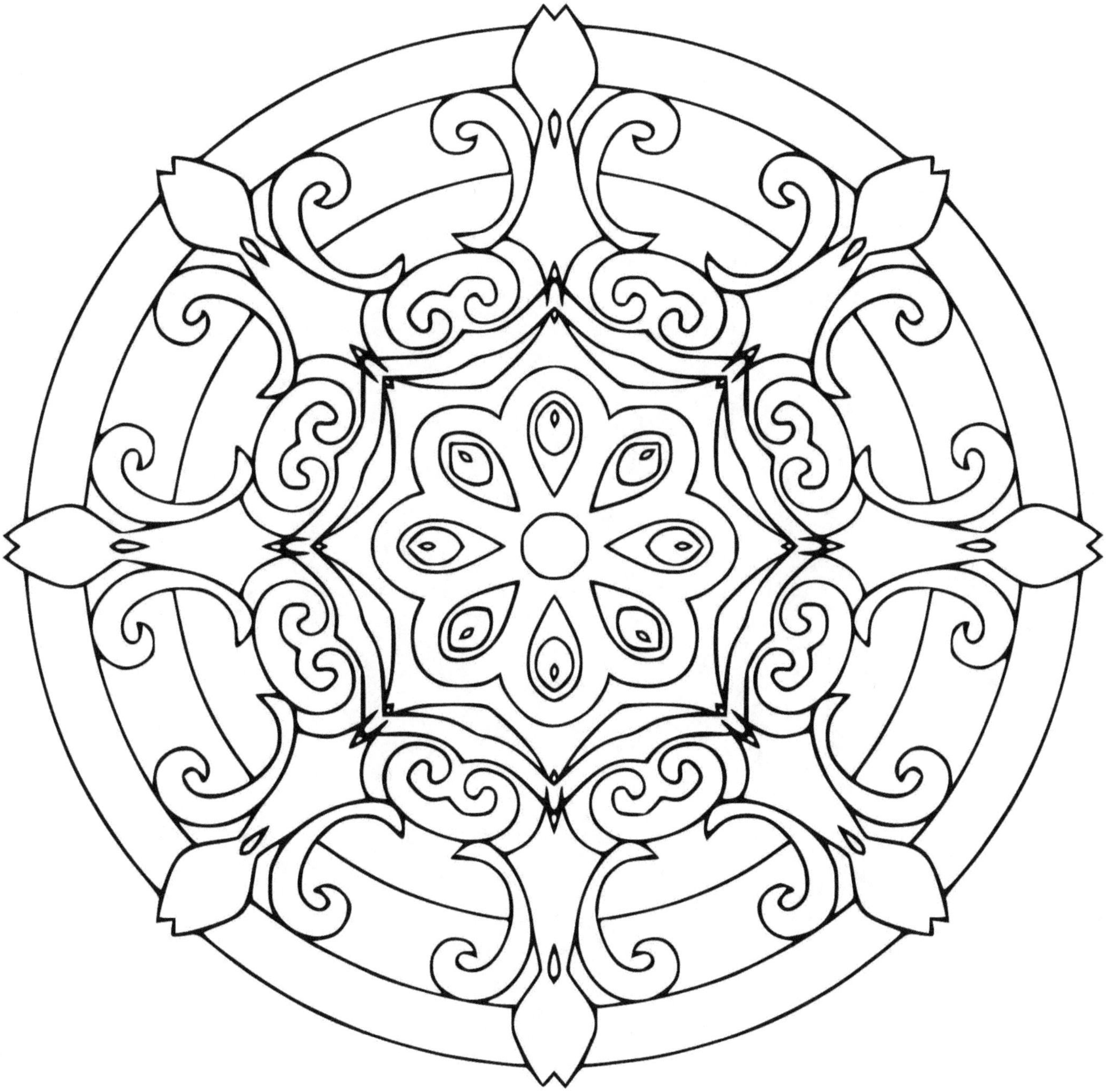

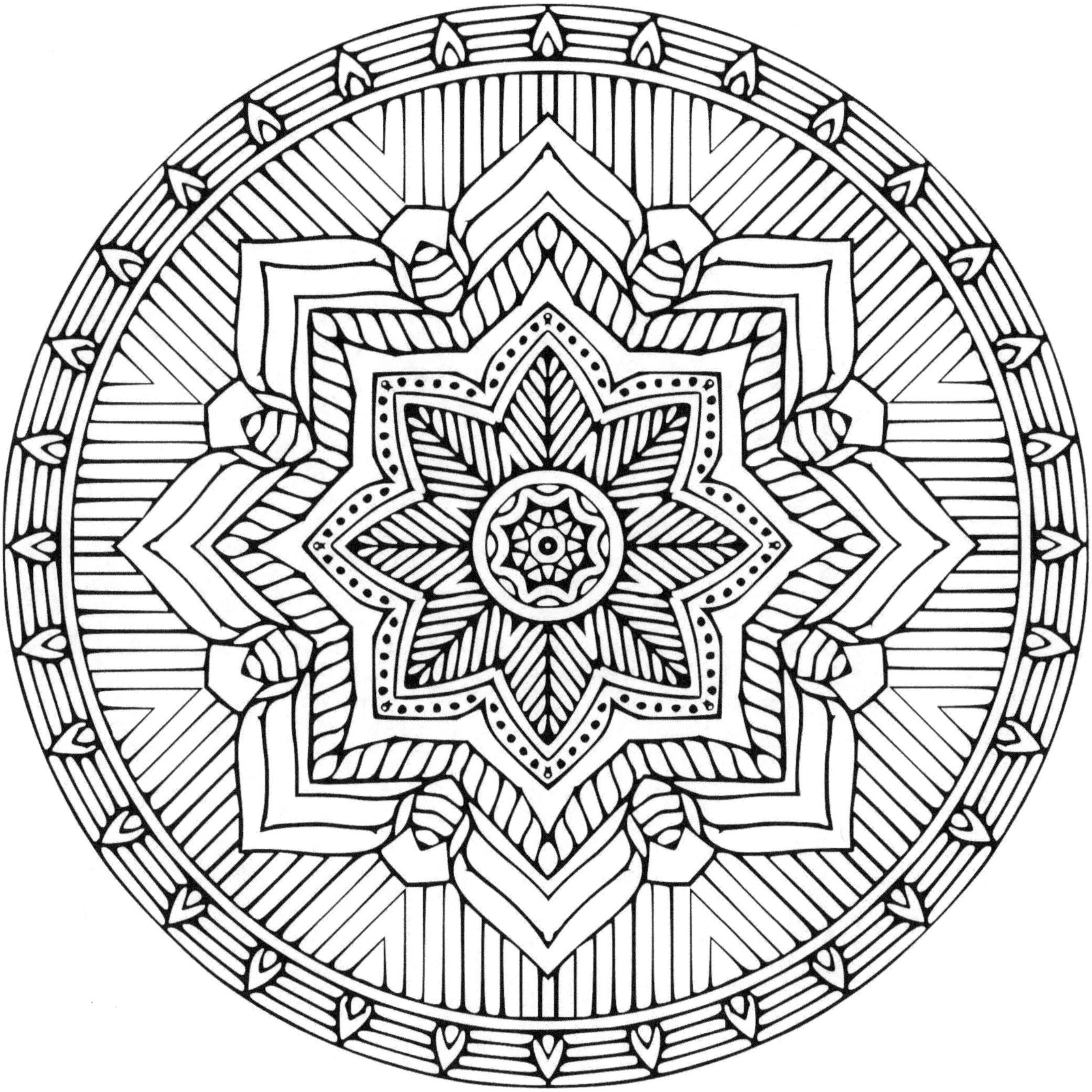

www.ingramcontent.com/pod-product-compliance
Lightning Source LLC
Chambersburg PA
CBHW080704190526
45169CB00006B/2236
* 9 7 8 1 5 3 4 8 9 8 5 5 4 *